the best path to - Northern wilderness is an . ♡ hiking trail!

Jim Buch

THE MINNESOTA
WALK BOOK

Volume I
Arrowhead Country

MINNESOTA WALK BOOK

James W. Buchanan
illustrated by Stephanie Torbert

A guide to Hiking and Cross-Country Skiing in Arrowhead Country

Volume I

NODIN PRESS

Minneapolis, Minnesota

ISBN 0-931714-36-2

Nodin Press, a division of Micawber's, Inc.
525 North Third Street,
Minneapolis, MN 55401

Dedicated to all those who travel
the trails of Arrowhead Country

About the Author

Jim Buchanan, a native of South Dakota, moved to Minnesota with his family while he was still in school. It was in Bemidji, while in his teens, that he became interested in the Minnesota woods.

He earned an A.S. degree from the North Dakota School of Forestry and also studied at the Michigan College of Mining and Technology at Houghton. Later, at Bemidji State College, he majored in the social and biological sciences and received a B.S. degree. Jim went on to earn a Master's Degree at the University of Minnesota at Duluth where he now resides with his family.

Jim Buchanan's education and work experiences have led him to write about his first interest, the foot trails of Minnesota. In each of the four tourism regions of the state he has found unexpected treasures.

Table of Contents

FOREWORD

With the advent of hiking and skiing as health components, the wish to trace the "moccasin trails" has blossomed into an increased need for up-to-date trail information. Jim Buchanan has been a skier/hiker all of this life and he has a keen knowledge and awareness of the many benefits of hiking and skiing the Arrowhead Country. This book will be of great benefit to those who wish to explore this gorgeous section of our state by foot. You will no doubt be renewed, refreshed, and inspired as you are exposed to the wonders that await you.

This veteran of backpacking lore who has been referred to as a "trail breaker" lends his spirit in this edition to assist you, the explorer, to find the essence of nature, and therefore, a slice of the real meaning of happiness.

Happy hiking and skiing!

Chuck Bloczynski
Regional Manager
Northeastern Region

INTRODUCTION

"Wandering through the country with a light pack is about the most interesting life imaginable, and perhaps the healthiest."

Calvin Rustrum

The purpose of this book is to list the necessities that are needed for walking and backpacking in the Minnesota Arrowhead region and Isle Royale, as well as to locate and describe the available trails.

Day hikers can get by with just a few light weight items in a day pack. Because day hikers do not pack camping gear or set up camp, they are able to cover greater distances in a day's hike than backpackers.

On the other hand, backpacking differs from day hiking in that the backpacker walks to a remote campsite to stay at least one night. All of the camping gear must be carried on his or her back, or to the campsite.

We've redesigned and updated this book to be taken along on your backpacking trips and walks to help you make the most of your outdoor enjoyment. It should be a personal book, since each trail can be a different experience every time it is walked.

Log space has been provided for notes, sketches, maps, and photos should you want to record your trips. The idea is that your notes and pictures will last longer than your memory of a particular trek.

I would like to thank the following agencies for help in preparation of this book:

Duluth Public Library
Minnesota Department of Natural Resources
Superior National Forest
University of Minnesota, Duluth

Walking in the Northwoods

"The Longest journey starts with just one step."

Tao Te Ching

When I first started hiking in the Arrowhead region there were very few people who used the rather limited number of walkable trails. Now nearly thirty years later there are more people getting out on an increasing number of trails. However, a region the size of the Arrowhead needs and should have even more foot trails to meet the expected rise in demand.

If there is to be further development of trail systems in the Arrowhead region, much of the impetus must come from trail users. Individuals and groups can do a great deal by contacting government and private agencies and expressing interest in more rural and urban trails. Because most people now live in cities, urban trails should be a part of any region's trail system. A nearby urban trail can provide the daily conditioning that is needed for a weekend or longer wilderness trek.

Rules for Safe Hiking and Backpacking

1. Plan your trip with care to details.
2. Have a map of the area that you intend to hike.
3. Inform a responsible person of where you are going and when you expect to return. Make a trip schedule, giving the approximate area you plan to be in for each day of the trip. Also, if you leave a vehicle at a trailhead, give its make and license number.
4. Do not hike alone.
5. Do not become separated from your pack.
6. Hike only on well-maintained designated trails.
7. When on the trail stay with your group.
8. When at a campsite use an established fire ring.
9. Burn all combustibles. Carry everything else out.
10. Put all fires out with water.
11. Do not cut living trees. It is against state and federal law.
12. If you cut dead wood, use a saw, not an axe.
13. Boil or treat all drinking water.
14. On the trail drink only from your canteen.
15. Carry extra food.
16. Do not tease or feed any animals.
17. Keep all food away from tents or sleeping bags.
18. Carry a signal device such as a whistle.
19. Bend down the barbs on all fishhooks.
20. Do not take chances swimming or diving in unknown waters.
21. Try out all equipment, clothing, and supplies at home.
22. Do not underestimate the changeable Minnesota weather. Take more clothes than you think you will need.
23. Wear protective eyewear to shield your eyes from brush, sparks, and sun glare.

Equipment, Clothing, and Supplies for Day Hiking

Besides wearing serviceable clothing and footwear, day hiking on most designated city and state park trails normally requires little in the way of equipment and supplies. The hiker usually can get by with rain gear, first aid kit, sun screen, insect repellant, and something to eat and drink.

All of these items can be carried in a fanny pack or small day pack. However, there are some things that sometimes are very handy to have on a longer distance day hike. Not so much in summer when there are no drastic changes in the weather, but for the spring and fall seasons when the weather rapidity change and put the hiker in danger of hypothermia. These items are best carried in an ample sized day pack with a capacity of 2,000 cubic inches or more.

Personal and Day Pack item check list:

☐ Billfold
☐ Canteen
☐ Extra socks
☐ Hat
☐ Hiking boots
☐ Insulated jacket
☐ Matches
☐ Nylon shell parka
☐ Pants
☐ Pocket knife
☐ Rain gear
☐ Shirt
☐ Sun glasses
☐ Moist towelettes
☐ Two pair of socks
☐ Watch
☐ Whistle

Clothing worn hiking should be of good quality and in serviceable condition. Avoid wearing old worn out clothing for the sake of economy.

Group Equipment and Supplies

- ☐ Compass
- ☐ First-aid kit
- ☐ Flashlight
- ☐ Insect repellent
- ☐ Lunch, if not in an urban area
- ☐ Lip ointment
- ☐ Map of area
- ☐ Sun screen

Optional Equipment

- ☐ Binoculars
- ☐ Camera and film
- ☐ Fishing tackle
- ☐ Hiking staff

As long as the day hiking is on well-marked, designated trails this should be a sufficient amount of gear to cover most eventualities. However, if the hike is in a remote area on poorly maintained trails, then at least a sleeping bag and bivouac sack or plastic tarp should be added in case of an unexpected overnight stay on the trail. The extra weight is cheap life insurance.

People who get into trouble in the woods are often underclothed, uninformed weekend sportsmen who rush into the wilds with gun or tackle in hand and without map or compass, not knowing where they are or where they are going.

Equipment, Clothing, and Supplies for Backpacking

Backpacking is another matter. A backpacker is a hiker who stays overnight on the trail. Therefore, he or she must carry all that is needed to camp out in comfort and safety.

Backpackers need all of the day hiking gear plus:

Clothing

☐ Change of clothing
☐ Gloves
☐ Hooded sweat shirt
☐ Insulated underwear-For sleeping or being stuck in the tent during foul weather.
☐ Stocking cap

Equipment

☐ A Backpack large enough to carry the extra equipment.
☐ Cook Kit
☐ Foam pad
☐ Nylon Cord
☐ Sewing Kit
☐ Sleeping bag
☐ Tent

Supplies

☐ Detergent
☐ Fire starters
☐ Food
☐ Iodine for water purification
☐ matches
☐ Paper towels
☐ Personal kit
☐ Toilet Tissue
☐ Scouring pads

Optional Equipment

- ☐ Folding saw
- ☐ Protective eyewear
- ☐ Single burner stove and fuel

To avoid leaving on a backpacking trip without taking some items of gear with you, make several copies of your list of clothing, equipment, and supplies. Carry one copy in your billfold and attach another to the outside of your backpack. Check off the items as they are packed. Separate clothing, equipment, and supplies by packing them in waterproof transparent plastic bags. Pack the heavier items toward the top of the pack. For comfort, pad the back of the pack with clothing. Attach sublists to each bag. Place these bags in the main cargo compartment of.the backpack. Carry extra plastic bags for soiled clothing, trash, or in case of damage to your backpack bags.

Use the outside pockets of the pack for items you want to have access to while on the trail, such as camera, compass, first-aid kit, flashlight, insect repellent, lunch, notebook and pen, and rain gear.

If your tent, sleeping bag, and pad are too bulky to be carried in the backpack, these items can be fitted to the outside of the pack. Use rubber tie-downs. The tent inside a waterproof bag can be attached to the top of the pack and the sleeping bag and pad, also in waterproof bags, to the bottom.

Once you have finished packing, try your backpack for balance and strap adjustment. If it feels right, weigh on a scale. The average man's pack should weigh somewhere around 45 pounds and the average woman's pack about 35 pounds. A child's pack should not be more than one-quarter of the child's weight. Try to keep the weight of your pack down. More backpacking trips have been ruined because of overloading than any other cause. Believe it!

Before going out on a backpacking trip it is a good idea to test your gear by setting up a camp in a safe place such as a public campground or even your back yard.

If you have any doubts about backpacking it would be wise to rent the gear from a reliable outfitter. Some backpackers who only take one or two trips a year prefer to rent, since they can have the use of the newest gear and there is no problem with storage.

Universities and colleges have outdoor education programs that offer backpacking trips as well as rent equipment.

Food

Food for day hikes and backpacking trips is a matter of personal choice. It is usually not very practical to cook while on a day hike. Meals on a backpacking trip are another matter. The foods you use while on a backpacking trip will depend on what you want, how much weight you are willing and able to carry, and how much time you want to spend in preparation.

For longer trips, some backpackers prefer freeze-dried foods. These are light-weight, easy to prepare, and involve no waste. Freeze-dried foods are available at outdoor outfitters. Other backpackers buy all their nutritional needs at the supermarket. Items such as dehydrated soups, cook-in-a-bowl cereals, soup in a cup, and dry beverage mixes are popular with backpackers, as is quick cooking oatmeal. The cost of supermarket food is often considerably less and it is almost as easy to prepare.

You can avoid much cooking and cleaning up by eating foods such as dried fruits, breads, crackers, nuts, cheese, and meats right out of the package.

Plan to eat mainly carbohydrates for breakfast and lunch, as they are easier to digest while on the move and they are a good source of quick energy. Cook your big meals at night when there is more time to prepare and enjoy them. In any case, those planning a backpacking trip would be well advised to try preparing and eating a wide range of foods at home before going out on a backpacking trip.

Do not depend upon gathering wild food because it can be a sometime thing. Its true that knowledge of edible plants, as well as other survival skills are always good skills to have in case of an emergency. On the other hand, the best way to handle an emergency is to prevent it from happening by being prepared. An experienced outdoor enthusiast will always have enough food for the trip plus a little more. Thus, packing in enough food with some extra provisions "just in case" is always a good idea.

Backpackers who go into wilderness areas such as the Boundary Waters Canoe Area may not carry in any nonburnable, disposable food and beverage containers. Play it safe and do not carry food containers that cannot be burned in the campfire or carried out with you.

The most important part of your equipment is you, physically and mentally. You may be able to buy or rent everything else, but you must have the strength, flexibility, agility, balance, endurance, and will necessary to lift, carry, climb, push, and pull your way through a backpacking trip. Therefore, before you start off on a backpacking trip make certain that you and the trip members are in good condition.

HYPOTHERMIA

Formerly known as exposure, hypothermia is one of the most common killers of outdoor recreationists. According to some estimates, every year more than a thousand Americans die from this condition.

Hypothermia occurs when the body loses heat faster than it can be produced. It becomes life threatening when the temperature of the inner core of the body is lowered to the point where it can no longer supply enough oxygenated blood to maintain vital organ function. In a matter of two or three hours death can occur from respiratory failure or cardiac arrest.

The first symptoms of hypothermia are uncontrollable shivering, drowsiness, confusion, and weakness.

Many people associate hypothermia with cold temperatures. However, the majority of hypothermia deaths occur in a temperature range between 30 and 50 degrees above zero. It is at these temperatures in the spring and fall that people are most likely to be outdoors improperly dressed and taking chances they would not take in midwinter.

Although important, air temperature is not the only factor in hypothermia. The other factors can be wind (wind chill kills), moisture (rain or fog), and exhaustion and dehydration.

Cold water next to the skin drains away body heat at a rapid rate. It is estimated that a person in wet clothing loses body heat about 25 times faster than a person wearing dry clothing. This is why hypothermia often occurs to tired, hungry, improperly dressed recreationists at low elevations during a spring or fall rain, or those in the mountains at the time of a summer shower.

Hypothermia can occur at relatively high temperatures in any region or climate. Many times outdoor recreationists are not aware of the danger and do not take preventive precautions.

MILD HYPOTHERMIA

This form of hypothermia can occur when people are exposed to moderately cold temperatures and then enter a warm shelter. When this happens the body rewarms the skin at the expense of the body's inner core, which results in a mild case of hypothermia. This type of hypothermia is not life threatening but it can cause drowsiness, and loss of judgement that could result in an accident. This condition does not improve very fast after the affected person comes in out of the cold. An hour after entering a warm room the temperature of the body's inner core can still be dropping. As a result, victims often have reported that they felt quite warm while their body's inner core was still losing heat. With this in mind it seems unwise to re-expose yourself to the cold until your inner core has had time to rise to normal temperatures, a process that could take several hours.

EXHAUSTION

This can be an important factor in hypothermia. Exhaustion is the result of energy depletion. A person in the outdoors is wholly dependent on a limited supply of usable body energy and the insulation values of his or her clothing.

The body moves on muscle power fueled by sugars derived from food (mainly carbohydrates) and water, which are converted by the body to glycogen. Part of this glycogen is stored in the liver and part is converted into sugar and stored in the muscles for quick use. Hikers travel on the energy of muscle sugar.

When these muscle sugars are burned, the byproducts of this combustion are heat, lactic acid, and carbon dioxide. Breathing removes the carbon dioxide through the lungs. The lactic acid and other detrimental products are dissipated throughout the whole body and can be flushed out only so fast.

Strenuous muscle activity can produce buildups of lactic acid and carbon dioxide faster than they can be dissipated. When this happens the body can become oversaturated, causing muscle failure or exhaustion. This condition will last until the body has time to automatically flush out the lactic acid buildup and disperse the carbon dioxide.

At rest the body can flush out about 30 percent of the lactic acid buildup in the first 5 minutes or so. But in the next 15 minutes of rest only about 5 percent will be removed. The best way to prevent the buildup of these harmful byproducts is to prevent their formation by traveling slower and taking rest breaks. Slower travel also allows for a better appreciation of the works of man and nature, and reduces the possibility of accidents. Tired people suffer a higher accident rate.

Lack of precaution leads to fatigue, which is followed by exhaustion, which paves the way for hypothermia, which can cause unconsciousness and death very quickly.

ENERGY

The amount of energy available to the body is determined by what food is eaten and when. Food eaten at night provides energy for the next morning. Breakfast becomes afternoon energy. Lunch is utilized at night. Foods like nuts, chocolates, and dried and fresh fruits provide the best sources of energy to be eaten while traveling.

Body heat is made possible by only one means, the metabolism of ingested food. You must eat to live. You cannot cram down a doughnut and a cup of coffee in the morning and put in a full day on the trail without feeling the effects of an inadequate fuel supply.

The body at rest can maintain its normal temperature for 24 hours on 1,700 calories. Depending on weather and terrain, a hiker can expend from 4,000 to 6,000 calories in the same time period. Unless these calories are replaced, the body's reserves will be depleted, and this will not leave enough energy to maintain a normal temperature of 98.6 degrees.

The first visible symptoms of exhaustion are poor reflex actions, poor control of arms and legs, the need for frequent and prolonged rest stops, and a dazed, careless attitude with decreased attention span.

HEAT LOSS

Radiation This is the leading cause of heat loss. An unprotected head may lose up to 40 percent of the body's total heat production at the temperature of 40 degrees Fahrenheit and 75 percent at 5 degrees Fahrenheit. If your feet are cold put on a wool stocking cap. If that is not enough protection pull your parka hood over that.

Conduction Contact with anything cooler than the temperature of your skin causes heat loss. This includes water, snow, metal, and air. Don't sit or lie on the ground. If you need to sit or lie down place a pad under you.

Convection The main purpose of clothing is to retain a layer of warm air next to the body. Any cooler air passing by the body tends to remove the protective warm air. The faster the wind (exchange of air) the greater the body heat loss. Always carry instant body shelter such as a parka or tent for protection from wind and wetness.

Perspiration and Respiration Evaporation of sweat from the skin contributes to heat loss. It is best to remain a little on the cool side of comfort in order to minimize the chances of sweating, so slow down and don't sweat.

Inhaling cool air and exhaling warm air also accounts for significant heat loss.

Wind Chill When the wind increases, even moderate temperatures become intolerable for body heat maintenance. Put on some type of body shelter such as additional clothing, a sleeping bag or a tent.

Water Chill Wet clothing can extract heat from your body 25 times faster than dry clothing. Protect your clothing from wet weather with a full rain suit. A poncho does not provide enough protection.

DEHYDRATION

Taking in enough fluids is very important because dehydration can be a major factor in hypothermia. Not only does the body lose moisture through perspiration, but there is additional loss caused by breathing cold, dry air. Together these can cause dehydration, which can reduce the volume of blood in the body. This means there is less oxygenated blood available for the functioning of vital organs such as the brain and heart.

Drink plenty of water. Over drink to be certain. Drink when you are not thirsty. If you only drink enough to quench your thirst it may not be enough and you still could become dehydrated. When you lose more than 10 percent of your body fluids you are beyond self help. The Israeli army requires soldiers to drink water at the start and during the course of any operation, even when they are not thirsty. They carry at least three canteens in the field. Taking in fluids is very important because our bodies are more than 70 percent water.

Urine color can be an indication of dehydration. The darker the color the more dehydrated you are.

Active outdoor recreationists should drink at least a gallon of liquid each day and more if they are involved in strenuous activity.

Don't drink untreated lake or river water which might contain Giardia lamlia, a dangerous bacteria! It is an intestinal parasite that can cause severe gastrointestinal problems. Because the organism is so widespread all groundwater should be considered to be contaminated. All water must be treated by boiling, filtering, or chemicals. If you're using chemicals, most authorities now consider iodine in its various forms to be the best way to treat water that may be contaminated with Giardia.

Do not drink alcoholic beverages, as this will expand the blood vessels, bringing body heat to the surface of the skin where it will be lost by radiation.

In the desert, those who lack experience can, if they panic, die four to seven hours after becoming lost. You can live without food much longer than you can without clean water.

AVOIDING HYPOTHERMIA

Hypothermia is more likely to affect children, slender people, dieters, and alcoholics, as well as those who are tired, hungry, thirsty, poorly dressed, or not in good physical or mental health. Most hypothermia victims are uninformed weekend outdoor recreationists who underestimate the dangers of prolonged exposure to rain, wind, and cold.

To avoid hypothermia, one should start out after a adequate meal the night before and a good night's rest as well as a full breakfast in the morning. Carry plenty of liquids and high energy food with you on the trail.

It is important to set reasonable goals and stick to them. Do not overextend yourself.

The first defense against hypothermia is proper clothing. Dress in clothing that is lightweight, loose, and in layers. This allows you to remove or put on clothing in order to be protected while at rest as well as while traveling. According to an experienced Alaskan brush pilot "If you can't sit down and fall asleep any time you're outdoors you are not dressed right. You shouldn't have to keep moving to stay comfortable."

The right clothing acts to cover the parts of the body that allow the greatest loss of body heat. The most important of these is the head, which radiates about 40 percent of the body's heat. The hands and wrists can lose 20 percent. Ten percent can be lost from the feet, and the torso and legs can lose about 30 percent the body's heat.

To both retain heat and stay dry calls for a combination of clothing that really works to wick perspiration away from the skin and provide insulation and protection against the effects of rain, snow, and wind. This requires three layers.

The first layer next to the skin is underwear made of polypropylene fibers. This material will only absorb 0.01 percent of its weight in water. It acts to wick moisture away from the skin. The second or middle layer is the insulation layer. It can be made up of wool shirts, insulated polyester jackets, vests, and pants. The third or outer layer consists of a parka and a pair of outer pants for protection against wind and water. The best material for this outer layer seems to be Gore-tex®. This is a fabric perforated with holes large enough to allow body moisture to escape in the form of vapor but too small to let in molecules of rainwater.

Because wind-driven rain is a major factor in the loss of body heat, it is very important to have rain gear that covers the head, neck, torso, and legs. Test your rain gear under a cold shower before venturing out.

If you're caught in a rainstorm, put on your rain gear before you become wet. Don your insulated clothing before you start to shiver. A good rule is to have enough clothing with you to allow you to survive a night in the open. For the northern states and high elevations any time during of the year this calls for a sleeping bag.

If the weather turns bad, such as falling temperatures and/or rain or snow with a strong wind, stop. Get under cover, even if it means turning back to a safe place or setting up a shelter on the trail.

Rest before becoming fatigued. Keep eating and drinking to keep the body's furnace functioning and feeding oxygenated blood to vital organs.

Remember: A good group leader knows when to quit! A man and his two teenaged sons started off on a backpacking trip into the mountains of Washington State. In the face of a rapidly developing spring blizzard the father refused to return to safety, saying that "Real men never turn back!" Although the sons survived their father's determination, the father did not. It would have been a much better thing for him and his family if he had turned back and lived. No recreational goal is worth risking a life.

FROSTBITE

Frostbite is the freezing of the skin or deeper tissues by exposure to extreme cold temperatures or the combination of low temperatures and high winds. To avoid frostbite, keep vulnerable parts of the body such as the head, neck, and the extremities protected by clothing, and watch for indications of frostbite such as white spots on the surface of the skin.

The best way to treat frostbite is to immerse the injured part in lukewarm water. Never rub the frostbite to warm it. Small bits of ice have formed in the affected cells, and rubbing the skin can damage the cells.

LOST

It is unlikely that you will become lost while on paved city park paths or well-used forest trails. However, your chances of becoming lost increase on a few less traveled wilderness trails.

My best advice is to turn back before you get lost. Don't trust your weekend navigation skills in the woods. Thus, if you see the trail's tread slowly disappear, it may be time to turn back. If legendary woodsmen and pioneers like Davy Crockett and Daniel Boone can lose their way, so can you.

If you are stranded in a wild area, remember the word: STOP. S is for the word *stop*. This is the first step in avoiding the urge to run off in a blind panic. T stands for *think*, put your brain into gear. Sit down and think back, mentally retracing your route. O is for *observe*, look around your surroundings, and use your map and compass to try to determine your location. Take an inventory of the contents of your pockets and pack. See what you have that will be helpful. Equally important is P which stands for *plan*. What will you do?

Don't forget to signpost your location with a brightly colored object such as a stocking cap or orange marking tape. Now, try to find the trail again, but always keep the signpost in sight. If you are not successful, return to the signpost. Consult your map, and if anyone was with you, try whistling. (By the way, any type of whistle is something you might want to bring along). Bivouac before nightfall, and enjoy an extra night in the wilderness.

In the morning, decide whether you should stay put and wait for help to arrive, try again to find the trail, or head out to the nearest road by using map and compass. In any case, do not abandon your backpack. If you have to get lost, getting lost while backpacking is probably the best time. As long as you keep your head, the contents of your pack should keep you alive until help comes.

PUBLIC TRANSPORTATION

Walking is, of course, nature's own individual transit system. However, getting to the hiking areas in this book will, for most of us, still require dependence upon the wheel and the internal combustion engine. For those walkers and backpackers who do not have their own cars, or do not wish to use their cars, we offer the following list of firms offering public transportation and group charters to the Arrowhead region.

Duluth Transit Authority
2402 West Michigan Street
Duluth, MN 55806
(218) 722-7283 or
(218) 722-4426
   Regular city service, plus group charters throughout the region.

Greyhound Bus Lines
2122 West Superior Street
Duluth, MN 55806
(218) 722-1605 or
(612) 371-3311
   Service between Duluth and the Twin Cities and between Duluth and Hibbing

Triangle Transportation Company
   Service between Duluth and International Falls and the Iron Range.

Turner Bus Lines
   Regular service between Duluth and Thunder Bay, Ontario via the North Shore.

   Both the Triangle Transportation Company and the Turner Bus Lines operate out of the Duluth Greyhound Bus Depot

Voyageur Bus Company
4861 Arnold Road
Duluth, MN 55803
(218) 724-1707
   Mini and full-size bus charter service throughout the region, from 10 passengers and up.

National Forest Trails

Chippewa National Forest

Marcell Ranger District

Located in north central Minnesota, the 640,000 acre Chippewa National forest grows forest products, protects water resources, manages Fish and wildlife and is a playground for visitors looking for outdoor recreation.

Suomi Hills Recreation Area

Suomi Hills Recreation Area, in the Marcell Ranger District, is a 5,000 acre management unit of the Chippewa National Forest that has been designated for non-motorized, dispersed outdoor recreation.

The parking lot for this recreational development is 19 miles north of Grand Rapids on State Highway 38, at the mile post 19 road marker.

The terrain at this recreation area is very hilly and heavily forested, with a number of small lakes among the hills.

For the advanced cross-country skiers there are 18 miles of challenging cross-country ski trails. These hilly trails can also be a good workout for hikers who are looking a higher level of exertion. In the summer, there is nothing like a brisk session hill of walking to increase your heart rate to the desired level.

Because there are a total of six wilderness campsites on the lakes along the trails, the Suomi Hills Recreation Area offers backpacking as well as day hiking opportunities.

For further information contact:
Chippewa National Forest
Marcell Ranger District
Marcell, MN 56657
(218) 832-3161

Superior National Forest

This large national forest is made up of 3 million acres of land and water. The forest is managed to develop its forest, water, and recreational resources and at the same time protect the environment.

Boundary Waters Canoe Area Wilderness (BWCA)

The BWCA makes up more than a million acres of the Superior National Forest, extending for almost 150 miles along our border with Canada. The BWCA is an undeveloped area of lakes and streams connected by portage trails. Primarily known for canoeing and fishing, However, the BWCA also contains a number of foot trails. Trails that are wholly or partially within the BWCA are subject to its special wilderness regulations.

According to the National Wilderness Preservation Act of 1964, a wilderness is a tract of undeveloped land with the following characteristics:

It is affected primarily by the forces of nature. Man is a visitor who does not remain. It may contain ecological, geological, or other features of scientific, educational, scenic, or historical value.

It possesses outstanding opportunities for solitude or a primitive and unconfined type of recreation.

It is an area large enough to warrant preservation and use in an unspoiled, natural condition.

Because the BWCA has more than 160,000 visitors each year, special regulations are necessary to preserve its wilderness characteristics. These are:

A wilderness permit is required from May 1 to September 30, if you plan to camp overnight. These are free and are available from any Superior National Forest office or from most resorts and outfitters located adjacent to the BWCA.

Non-burnable, disposable food and beverage containers are not permitted in the wilderness.

Party size is limited to no more than 10 people.

Motorized travel is not permitted on hiking trails.

Open fires are allowed within the steel firegrate at designated campsites only, unless specifically authorized on the permit.

On those trails that do not have camping facilities, camping is allowed only when .25 mile from another group or site and at least 100 feet from the trail, portage, or lakeshore.

Lakes scattered along the trails provide drinking water, but carry a canteen for those long stretches between lakes. Boil or treat all drinking water. Do not wash dishes in or near a lake or stream.

Use toilet facilities at existing campsites or dig a latrine at least 100 feet from the trail or any water source and cover it before leaving.

Use only dead wood for fires and tent poles. Use cord instead of nails or wire.

Be sure to fully extinguish your fire before leaving camp.

Leave a clean campsite for those who follow by burning or carrying out all refuse.

Before departing, check with a permit issuing station on the current condition of the trail.

For further information contact:
Superior National Forest
P.O. Box 338
Duluth, MN 55801
(218) 720-5342

Gunflint Ranger District

The Border Route Trail

The Border Route Trail is a 75-mile-long trail along the Canadian border from the Gunflint Trail (Cook County Road 12) to the Grand Portage Trail (the main trail of the Grand Portage National Monument). The trail's construction and maintenance is a project of the Minnesota Rovers Outing Club with the cooperation of public agencies, private organizations, and area landowners.

Some of the main accesses to the Border Route Trail:

From the Gunflint Trail (Cook County Road 12)

The road to Gunflint Lodge and Heston's Resort

43.1 miles from Grand Marais

The road to Borderland Lodge

43.8 miles from Grand Marais

At the parking lot for the Magnetic Rock Trail

46.5 miles from Grand Marais

From the Arrowhead Trail (Cook County Road 16).

At a parking lot this side of the bridge between McFarland Lake and Little John Lake.

The Rovers guidebook *The Border Route Trail* has divided the Border Route Trail into three sections:

1. The Gunflint Lake Section (west). According to the guide, this west end is the best section for cross-country skiing. The Border Route Trail in this section is connected to a number of cross-country ski trails, many of which are tracked by area resort crews.

2. The BWCA Section (middle). The guidebook reports that this section of trails is not suitable for cross-country skiing because parts are too narrow, or steep with sharp turns, and there many rocks and deadfalls. However, it is considered to be a good trail section for snowshoeing as well as backpacking.

3. Pigeon River Section (east). This section is rated by the guidebook as good for backpacking, snowshoeing, and wilderness cross-country skiing.

At the present time the Border Route Trail can be described as primitive. In places the trail is poorly signed and blocked by downed trees, making it difficult for hikers to follow. However, at the present time it is a worthwhile trail for experienced hikers who have a sense of adventure and a desire for solitude.

It is this writer's hope that the Border Route Trail in the future will be easier to traverse due to increased use by recreationists and additional work on trail improvements. The Minnesota Rovers are looking for help in developing this important trail.

If you would like to volunteer your services for construction or maintenance on this very important trail please contact:
Edward K. Solstad
Minnesota Rovers
P.O. Box 14133
Dinkytown Station
Minneapolis, MN 55414
(612) 822-0569

For further information contact:
Forest Service
District Ranger
Box 308
Grand Marais, MN 55801
(218) 387-1750

Minnesota Department of Natural Resources
500 Lafayette Road
Box 40
Saint Paul, MN 55146
1 (800) 652-9747 or
1 (612) 296-6699

Caribou Rock Trail

This trail is off of Forest Road 148 about two miles east of the Gunflint Trail (County Road 12). The trail is on the north side of Hungry Jack Lake. On the official state highway map the grid location is Q-5. There is a sign marking the start of the trail.

Caribou Rock Trail is fairly level at first, then it starts going upwards. The forest here is mainly red pine, aspen, birch, and balsam fir. You have to watch where you place your feet as the path is rough and rocky and there are many exposed roots. Toward the end however, the trail the tread becomes a grassy, pine-needle-covered path.

The trail ends up at Caribou Rock, a large rock outcropping that slants toward West Bearskin Lake, and offers a view of the lake that is well worth the uphill walk.

Gneiss Lake Trail

Gneiss Lake Trail (pronounced with a hard 'G') is U.S. Forest Service Trail No. 145. It begins almost at the end of the Gunflint Trail. Its state highway map grid location is P-5. About one mile east of the End of Trail Campground, a road turns to the right off the Gunflint Trail. Gneiss Lake Trail is approximately two miles in length, and its condition ranges from good to fair, as it swings over ridges and through low spots. This is a trail for boots and scratch-resistant clothing. You may not like the wet footing, but you will enjoy the view of Gneiss Lake. Along the path you should also be watchful for moose and other wild creatures.

Honeymoon Bluff Trail

This trail starts about 100 yards east of the Flour Lake Campground on Forest Road 172. The road turns right (east) off of the Gunflint Trail (County Road 12) about 25 miles out of Grand Marais.

Parking for this trail is on the north side of Forest Road 172. On the official state highway map its grid location is Q5.

At the start the trail is quite level, but after a short distance it begins to climb. A sign warns parents to keep small children in hand while walking on the steep sections of this trail.

After passing under a powerline there is a gradual uphill walk aided at steep places by staircases made from railroad ties. Wet places on the trail are crossed on planking. The trail ends on top of the bluff amid a forest of jack pine and white spruce. There is a gravel-covered walkway around the top of the bluff in the form of a loop. A turn to the left on the loop leads to an overlook with an east view of Wampus Lake. Swinging right on the loop brings the walker to the cliffs overlooking Hungry Jack Lake. To the northwest of this point, West Bearskin Lake can be seen. The edge of the cliff is protected by a rail fence.

Kekekabic Trail

(see Kawishiwi Ranger District)

Lima Mountain Trail

This short but scenic hiking trail is 22 miles north of Grand Marais. Take the Gunflint Trail (County Road 12) for 20 miles. Turn to the left (west) on Forest Road 152. Follow this road for two miles. The Lima Mountain Trail starts at the junction of Forest Roads 152 and 315. On the official state highway map the grid location is Q-6.

This trail is a mile long and ends up at the site of the Lima Mountain fire lookout tower. In the past there were many fire towers in the Superior National Forest. Eventually, however, aircraft patrolling replaced the lookout towers for locating fires, and all the towers, including the Lima Mountain Tower, were torn down. The Lima Mountain Tower was removed in 1978.

The fire tower site is 2,238 feet above sea level and has a panoramic view of the Misquah Hills to the west.

Short trails like this one offer people an opportunity to experience the scenic beauty of our forests away from roadside distractions.

Magnetic Rock Trail

The Magnetic Rock Trail, a good family hiking trail, starts 37 miles northwest of Grand Marais. On the state highway map its grid location is P-5. It is designated U.S. Forest Service trail No. 144. This trail goes east from the Gunflint Trail about 2 miles south of the Sea Gull Forest Service Station. There is no place to park a car at this trail's head, but the parking lot of the Kekekabic Trail (see Kawishiwi Ranger District) is less than a quarter of a mile south on the other side of the road.

This two mile trail bypasses some low areas, goes uphill, and follows ridges to its destination, a huge magnetic monolith that looks like one of the standing pieces of Stonehenge. It is a very unique rock. The trail is in good condition and passes through some interesting country. Plan to spend the better part of the day there to really see it.

South Lake Trail

The South Lake Trail is a four mile trail from the Gunflint trail to the east end of South Lake. It is designated as Forest Service Trail 132. The trail begins directly north of the Rockwood Lodge on Poplar Lake, about 30 miles from Grand Marais. The state highway map grid location is Q-6. The South Lake Trail was once used for motor vehicles. Now it is a foot trail.

The most prominent features of this part of northeastern Minnesota are the ridges that rise above the rest of the landscape. These ridges are generally on an east-west line. They are composed of a hard diabase rock of volcanic origin that has withstood the effects of erosion, while the softer slate rock has been worn down to form valleys between the ridges. Because of the tilt of the rock structure, the ridges have gently sloping south faces and steeply sloping north faces. In profile these ridges look like the cutting edge of a saw, giving them the name "Sawtooth Mountains."

The trail follows the south shore of Birch Lake from west to east at the bottom of the north face of a long east-west ridge. When the trail goes around the east end of Birch Lake, it heads north. It then crosses a ridge going up the gentle south slope and down the steeper north side for a half-mile. Here the trail touches the east end of East Otter Lake, which like most lakes in this area, is an elongated lake on an east-west axis. There is a small stream here. The trail then traverses a half-mile ridge to Partridge Lake. The remainder of the trail is a mile-long crossing to the east end of South Lake.

South Lake is a popular canoe route, so you can expect to see canoe parties on this lake. In general, it is not a good idea to plan to camp on lakes that are on main canoe routes for the campsites could be crowded, especially if the lake does not have islands to camp on.

The last part of the South Lake Trail is within the BWCA. If you plan to camp at East Otter, Partridge, or South Lakes, have your travel permit with you. The nearest Forest Service campground is at Iron Lake, four miles west of Birch Lake Scenic Vista. (Use Fisher Map No. 114 for this trail.)

For maps and further information on Gunflint Ranger District trails contact:

Superior National Forest
Gunflint Ranger District   Grand Marais, MN 55615
P.O. Box 308   (218) 387-1750

Isabella Ranger District

Arrowhead Creek Trail

This easy walking trail is located northeast of Isabella. From Isabella take Forest Road 172 east for a mile. Turn north (left) on Forest Road 369 for six miles and then east (right) on Forest Road 173. The trail access is from the two roads from the south that junction onto 173 on either side of Arrowhead Creek. The creek is signed, the trail is not. The second, most easterly of the two roads ends at the Arrowhead Creek Trail parking lot about a quarter of a mile south of 173. On the official state highway map the location is 0-7.

The Trail

Arrowhead Creek Trail is a five-mile-long loop trail developed from old logging roads. It is now maintained as a foot trail for use by hikers, hunters, bird watchers, photographers, or anyone interested in experienceing part of the natural world on foot. Narrow foot bridges cross Arrowhead Creek to keep vehicles off the trail.

This trail is on level, firm ground through a lowland area with a wide range of wildlife habitats that include mature pine plantations, mixed northern hardwoods, and lowland brush.

Some of the wildlife species that are common in this trail area include moose, white-tailed deer, bear, red squirrels, and ruffed grouse. During the fall migration the Arrowhead Creek Trail area may provide feeding areas for that strange-looking bird, the woodcock, who uses his long flexible bill to probe for earthworms in moist soil.

Because the Arrowhead Creek Trail is so near to the town of Isabella and local resorts it has become a very popular place ot take a walk in the woods.

A BWCA permit is not required for this trail.

Divide Lake Trail

This trail starts at the Divide Lake Campground, which is five miles east of Isabella on Forest Road 172. On the official state highway map its grid location is 0-7.

The campground has three campsites and a separate day-use area, which includes a picnic area and a boat launching ramp. It is also the trailhead to the Divide Lake Trail.

Divide Lake is named after the Lauretian divide and runs along a ridge on its north side. Water from the north side of the divide flows to Hudson's Bay, while that from the south side moves toward the Atlantic Ocean. It is a 69-acre lake.

The Trail

The Divide Lake Trail starts from the boat access point and is marked with a sign. Most of its two miles around Divide Lake is within sight of the lake's waters. Along the trail there are a number of rest benches at scenic overlooks, that inclued views of adjacent 63-acre Tanner Lake and the 13-acre Crosscut Lakes.

Among some of the features of the trail are wild flowers, bird's nests, and stumps of trees felled by beaver. There are also man-made rock structures extending across the mouths of streams. They serve to prevent the lake's planted trout from migrating out of the lake. They also act as bridges for people and wildlife.

For those who are looking for a remote place to camp there is a single campsite on Blueberry Point on the lake's south shore.

The trail ends on Forest Road 172 a short distance east of the Divide Lake Campground.

A BWCA permit is not required for this trail.

Eighteen Lake Hiking Trail

Eighteen Lake camping area is northeast of the town of Isabella, which is on State Highway 1 about halfway between Illgen City on the North Shore Highway 61 and Ely. From Isabella, take Forest Road 172 east to the junction with Forest Road 369. Turn north on 369 for about a mile and a half where there is a road on the west (left) side of 369 into Eighteen Lake camping area. Eighteen Lake has 113-acres. On the official state highway map its grid location is 0-7.

To avoid damage to the lake's shoreline, the camping area is set well back. There are three campsites. Each site has its own looped driveway, wide enough to park a trailer. There is also additional space in each site for tents and RV's. Each site is shielded from the other sites by large pines. Each site has a fire grate, picnic table, and access to toilets. Firewood is available. There are no user fees. Public use of the Eighteen Lake campground is light.

For day-use recreationists there is a large parking lot near the lake's shoreline.

The Trail

The Eighteen Lake hiking Trail is a two-and-a-half mile long loop trail around the lake. The topography offers a variety of hiking experiences. There are ridgetop views of the forest and lakes, as well as planked walkways where you may have close up inspections of wetland plants and animals without getting your feet wet.

The forest cover changes with the lay of the land. Red pine, maple, and birch grow on the dry ridges, while there is mainly white cedar in the bogland.

Camping areas such as Eighteen Lake are grand places for an outdoor recreational weekend. It is possible to camp, fish, canoe, hike, pick berries, and take long naps: all while staying at one place.

A BWCA permit is not required for this trail.

Flathorn Lake Trail

This two mile trail starts at the Flathorn Lake Picnic Area. From Isabella take State Highway 1 west for six miles and turn north on Forest Road 177 for a mile. The location of Flathorn Lake Picnic Area on the official state highway grid is 0-7.

The picnic area has tables and grills, vault toilets, a water system (hand pumps), and refuse receptacles. The waterfront offers fishing access and a swimming beach, but no lifeguard.

The Trail

The Flathorn Lake Trail is a two mile semi-loop trail around Flathorn Lake, which is a 63-acre lake. The trail starts at the north end of the picnic ground and ends on a road at the former site of the Environmental Learning Center. However, a short distance to the left there is a trail that goes into the woods and over a bridge back to the Flathorn Lake Picnic Area. This sort of makes the Flathorn Lake Trail a loop trail.

The trail had been an important educational tool for the Environmental Learning Center.

Along its two miles there are a wide range of forest types and land forms that help to create a number of widlife habitats, which attracts many species of animals to this area. A person with an active interest in nature could spend the better part of a day at Flathorn Lake.

A BWCA permit is not required to hike this trail.

Hogback Lake Hiking Trail

The trailhead for this six mile-long trail system is at the Hogback Lake Picnic Area 12 miles east of Isabella on Forest Road 172. On the official state highway map the grid location is 0-7.

In the picnic area there are five picnic sites, pit toilets, a refuse depository, and a boat launching site for Hogback and Canal Lakes. This is a day-use area; camping is not permitted. However, there are five primitive campsites along the trail, each having a cleared tent space, a fire grate, and a latrine.

Hogback, Canal, Scarp, and Steer lakes are designated as trout lakes and are stocked yearly with rainbow trout. A Minnesota trout stamp is required to fish in these trout lakes.

Hogback Lake's name comes from the long, narrow ridges, some up to 70 feet high, which dominate the landscape. The hogbacks are rock formations created by differential erosion. This is a geological process by which softer rock is eroded at a faster rate than the harder rock. In this case the process leaves the harder rock standing in place as narrow ridges.

The Trails

The Hogback Lake Trails start east of the picnic area and follow the shoreline of 44-acre Hogback Lake by the boat access, continuing on in a southeastern direction to join the two loops that make up most of this trail system.

The northern loop circles Scarp Lake. This is a 43-acre lake with two campsites. Both of which are accessible by spur trails off the main trail. One campsite is on a promontory at the midpoint of the north shore. The other is on the west side of the lake. This loop passes by the south shore of 18-acre Mound Lake as well as the south shore of Hogback Lake and the northeast shore of Canal Lake.

The southern loop is joined to the northen loop at two junctions. The west junction is south of 10-acre Canal Lake and the east junction is south of the midpoint of the south shore of Scarp Lake. The west side of the loop follows the north arm of 93-acre Lupus Lake before turning to pass by the north shore of the east arm of the lake where there is a campsite. Continuing northeast, the east side of the loop joins the north loop.

There is also a side trail from the east side of the north loop that turns to the east, passing the northwest corner of Steer Lake before reaching Forest Road 7.

This is another of the Superior National Forest developments that offers a number of recreational options. From the Hogback Picnic Area it is possible to have a picnic, try angling for trout, photograph the natural world, canoe or boat, bird watch, pick berries, day hike, or backpack to a back country campsite near the shoreline of a lake.

A BWCA permit is not required for this trail.

McDougal Lake Campground Hiking Trail

McDougal Lake Campground is 10 miles west of the town of Isabella on State Highway 1. Turn south on Forest Road 106. On the official state highway map its grid location is 0-7.

There are separate camping and day use areas. For campers there are 21 campsites, each with a table and fire rings. Nearby are pit toilets, trash cans, and hand water pumps.

The day use area has two picnic sites, each with a table and a pedestal grill. Next to the day use area parking lot is the boat launching ramp. Nearby is a swimming beach. Lifeguards are not provided.

The Trail

This is a mile-long loop trail starting and ending at the same place near the boat launching ramp.

After following the shoreline of 262-acre McDougal Lake for a short distance, the trail turns and enters a young birch forest, typical of the forest growth that follows clear cut logging or fire.

An advantage of hiking short trails like the McDougal Lake Campground Hiking Trail is that the hiker can take enough time to look at the smaller plants that make up a good part of the forest as well as the trees.

McDougal Lake Campground lends itself to a variety of outdoor activities such as camping, picnicking, swimming, boating or canoeing, fishing, and day hiking all at one place. Family groups and others have been known to return to places like this year after year.

Because McDougal Lake Campground is outside of the BWCA a permit is not required here.

Pow Wow Trail

This primitive trail system lies north of the town of Isabella. From Isabella take Forest Road 172 east for a mile and a half. Turn left (north) on Forest Road 369 for about six miles. At the next junction turn northwest on Forest Road 373 for another six miles to where the road cuts into Forest Road 377. Turn right (northeast) on Forest Road 377 and proceed to the trailheads on the extreme end of F.R. 377. On the official state highway map the grid location is 0-6.

The trail is named after Pow Wow Lake, a 21-acre lake that has a maximum depth of 42 feet. The main game fish here is the northern pike. At the present time Pow Wow Lake is not accessible, as it is in the trail's closed off eastern loop.

The trailhead parking area was once the site of Forest Center, a town with a population of 250. It served as Logging Camp #3 for the Tomahawk Timber Company from the early 1950s until 1965.

After the logging operations were closed down, a trail system was put together incorporating logging roads with new foot trails. This created a system designed to provide a wilderness experience in an area within the BWCA that is not on a canoe route.

The Pow Wow Trail is a primitive trail lacking the refinements normally expected in a forest service trail system, such as bridged streams and well-marked routes. The Pow Wow is not an average hiking trail. Anyone planning to hike it should have had considerable wilderness travel experience. The most favorable times to hike this trail would be in late spring or early fall. Insects can be a problem in midsummer.

Cross-country skiing is difficult on the Pow Wow Trail, because the access roads are not plowed and it might take a full day of skiing to reach the trailheads.

In the past years the Pow Wow Trail had both an east and west loop. Now due to very difficult flooding problems partly caused by beaver damming, the east loop trail has been closed. It is hoped that this loop will be reopened sometime in the future, because it offers a lot of interesting back country.

Anyone planning a hiking trip on the Pow Wow Trail will need a reliable compass and an accurate topographic map. Three maps that can be used to hike the trail are: Fisher F-4, Mckenzie [5]19, and USGS quadrangles Isabella Lake and Quadga Lake.

The West Loop

Heading northwest from the parking area south of Isabella Lake, the trail crosses the bridge over the Isabella River. The trail's direction is north for two miles on an old logging road to a trail junction. A left (west) turn is taken on another old logging road for the next five miles. Except for Marathon Lake the small lakes along this stretch of trail are without campsites. This part of the trail ends in a north turn.

From here most of the rest of the west loop is new trail construction. It is a narrow, rough track that looks more like a backpacking trail than the logging roads. Along this part of the loop there are a number of small lakes with wilderness-type campsites.

The topography here varies from ridges of exposed rock to mucky lowlands.

Because this area has been logged many times, the forest cover ranges from mature forest to newly planted seedlings.

The Pow Wow Trail area is moose country. The trail, expecially the sections of old logging road, usually have a fine display of moose tracks.

The Pow Wow Trails are within the BWCA. Backpackers must obtain overnight permits from the Superior Forest Service offices. Day hikers may use permits for day use, which are issued by resorts and others who are co-operators with the Superior Forest Service.

For those who have the right gear and the know-how to use it, the Pow Wow Trails provide a way into northeastern Minnesota's natural world.

White Pine Interpretive Trail

This quarter-mile-long, self-guided nature trail is in the Superior National Forest White Pine Picnic Area. The picnic area is named for the large grove of huge white pine that stands tall above the surrounding second growth forest.

White Pine Picnic Area is on Lake County Road 2 about 25 miles north of Two Harbors. On the official state highway map its grid location is N-8.

The Trail

The White Pine Interpretive Trail circles through a quarter mile of the picnic area with signs pointing out features of the natural world at stations along the trail. A self-guided tour is found in brochures available in a container at the parking lot.

White Pine Picnic Area is a good place to take a break from traveling, have a picnic in the woods, and to learn a few things about northern forests while walking the nature trail.

For a map and further information on Isabella Ranger District trails contact:
Superior National Forest
Isabella Ranger District
P.O. Box 207
Isabella, MN 55607
(218) 323-4255

Kawishiwi Ranger District Trails

Angleworm Trail

The Angleworm Trail is about 14 miles northwest of Ely off the Echo Trail Forest Road 116. The trail was built in the 1930's to provide access to a Forest Service cabin on Crooked Lake, and was formerly known as the Crooked Lake Trail. At the present time the trail east of Angleworm Lake is not passable. It is to be hoped that in the future this and other old trails in the BWCA will be put back into hiking condition.

The trail starts off at Echo Trail parking lot in a northeasterly direction. After a mile of fairly level terrain, the trail drops down into the valley of Spring Creek. The creek valley is very interesting.

From looking at it on maps, aerial photos, and on the site, it seems to be a small rift valley, that is, a valley along the trace of a geological fault. The creek is used as part of a cross-country ski trail during the winter.

The Angleworm Trail crosses Spring Creek on a well-built bridge. All wet places on this trail are crossed by new, solid constructions. After crossing the creek the trail continues up a ridge on its northeasterly course for a mile or so. It then turns north to bypass a swampy area. After going around this area, it returns to a northeasterly course headed for the southern end of Angleworm Lake. The trail here joins the main part of the trail, which is a loop around Angleworm, Home, and Whisky Jack Lakes. The trail is a narrow goat path that twists up and down while crosses a number of ridges.

Paralleling the west side of 148-acre Angleworm Lake, the trail follows along on on high ridges, passing by several campsites. About halfway up the lake the trail swings away from the lake, heading north to a scenic overlook. Past this high point, it turns toward the northeast, and after a stream crossing, follows the north shore of 85-acre Home Lake, where there is a campsite. After crossing the Home Lake to Gull Lake portage, the trail swings south away from Home Lake and along ridges to a scenic overlook above a small lake.

Following the ridgeline the trail continues south to another scenic overlook before turning to the west to pass by the south shore of 26-acre Whisky Jack Lake, where there is a campsite. Continuing west past Whisky Jack Lake the trail heads for the east side of Angleworm Lake and follows it around to rejoin the trail junction southwest of the lake.

Because the Angleworm Trail is only 14 miles long it might seem possible to day-hike it. However, because of the up and down nature of the trail, most hikers would do better to at least make it an overnight backpacking trip. Thus, it would make a great weekend backpacking trip. Some recreationists only hike part way around the loop until they come to a campspite, where they stay for several days. There is no law that says every trail has to be walked the full distance.

Angleworm Trail is within the Boundary Waters Canoe Area, and visitors are subject to its special regulations. Permits must be carried. The nearest campground is at Fenske Lake. (Use Fisher map No. 112 for this trail.)

Bass Lake Trail

This interesting 5.6-mile-long loop trail is located off of the Echo Trail (County Road 116). To reach this trail from Ely go east on Highway 169 past the Forest Service Voyageur Visitor Center. You might want to stop at the Center for current trail information. Stay on 169 and turn off on County Road 88, which will take you north and then west to the junction with the Echo Trail (County Road 116). It is another three miles to the Bass Lake parking lot. On the official state highway map its grid location is M-6. It is signed and on the right side of the road.

Although this trail is only 5.6 miles long, a hiker should allow at least four hours to complete the loop. Those who have an interest in geology and/or botony may want spend a full day or more because the trail offers a number of interesting things to see.

Bass Lake Trail is a rough track requiring a pair of sturdy hiking boots. Walking shoes made for paved surfaces will not do.

The trail loops around four lakes. These are Low Lake, Bass Lake, Dry Lake, and Little Dry Lake. Before 1925 only Bass Lake and Low Lake existed.

As part of a logging operation a sluiceway was built to float logs from Bass Lake to Low Lake. In 1925, the gravel ridge between the two lakes became saturated as a result of seepage from the sluiceway. The gravel ridge gave way, opening a gully 250 feet wide through which much of the water of Bass Lake poured into Low Lake. The water level of Bass Lake dropped 55 feet. The result was three smaller lakes where there was once one lake. In addition, 250-acres of former lake bottom was opened to colonization by land plants. Botanists are interested in newly exposed lake bottoms because the regeneration of vegetation is similar to that which takes place on the edges of receding glaciers.

Bass Lake Trail heads north from the parking lot for 600 yards. After going under a power line, the trail divides as it enters the loop that makes up most of its length. Turning to the left there is a descent down to part of the old lake bottom. After passing over a creek there is a climb up to a ridge, and after a mile or so on the ridge the trail crosses the bridge over Dry Falls. Past that the trail crosses the portage between Dry Lake and Bass Lake. The trail then goes up a hill and down into a grove of red pine where a wooden post marked with a teepee symbol indicates a side trail to two campsites on Bass Lake.

The main trail continues in the old lake bottom until it goes up across an open ridge to a high scenic viewpoint. After this high point there is descent back to the old lake bottom. The trail then leads around to the east end of Bass Lake and to the site of the 1925 washout. After crossing the gully area it turns to the south and passes over a stream on a Forest Service bridge. From here on, the path follows a southwest bearing, over ridges and across an old lake bed until it returns to the starting place.

A BWCA permit is not required to hike this trail.

Cummings Lake Trail

Cummings Lake Trail takes off from Forest Road 644, three miles south of the Echo Trail Forest, Road 116. It is a five-mile trail in generally good walking condition. The direction of the trail is from east to west.

The trail leaves the parking lot and proceeds through gently rolling hills that are forested with a second growth of mixed forest. After about three-quarters of a mile from the road, a branch trail goes north. This is a quarter-mile-long trail that ends at a small campsite on the south end of Slim Lake.

Slim Lake is a rather long, narrow, north-south lake. It is 315-acres in area, and has seven miles of shoreline. From talking with campers at the lake, I understand that it has walleyes, northerns, and panfish.

The main trail continues west and is joined by an old logging road. A short distance later, the trail crosses a small stream and passes between two small lakes. The one on the north is Coxey Pond. It has 128-acres of surface and 2.2 miles of shoreline. The lake on the south is Silaca Lake. This 40-acre lake is the smaller of the two, and has less than a mile of shoreline. Part of the shoreline of both lakes appears to be favorable for angling. The trail then crosses a small stream that flows from Coxey Pond into Silaca Lake. After another mile-and-a-half, the trail forks, with the trail left heading west to the shore of Cummings Lake, and the right trail going north to a cleared area that was once the site of a Forest Service cabin. This is a good place to camp. Cummings lake is a large lake with an area of 1,625-acres and 25 miles of shoreline. It has lake trout and northern pike.

This trail is within the BWCA and is subject to its regulations. (Use Fisher map No. 112 for this trail).

Kekekabic Trail

The Kekekabic Trail runs 38 miles from its trailhead at the parking lot off of the Gunflint Trail, 45 miles northwest of Grand Marais, to the trailhead parking lot off of Fernberg Road, 26 miles east of Ely. On the state highway map the grid location of the Gunflint trailhead is P-6 and that of the Fernberg Road trailhead is O-6.

The trail is named after Kekekabic Lake from the Ojibway name KeKeequabic, which means Hawk Cliff Lake.

Use Fisher Maps 113 and 114 for this trail.

Both trail heads are signed and have parking lots.

It is sometimes possible to arrange transportation to or from the trail heads through the resort operators at both ends. Gunflint Lodge near the eastern end has a campground and also rents cabins. Its dinning room is a great place to have a meal. They could provide transportation to or from Grand Marais, which is serviced by public transportation. Near the Fernberg Road trailhead, Kawishiwi Lodge has similar facilities and can provide transportation to or from Ely, also on a public bus route.

A little planning and advance correspondence could relieve the hiker of any anxiety over an unattended car left parked in the woods for a week or more. This would also save making a round trip over one of Minnesota's toughest hiking trails.

And it is tough! An experienced backpacker that I talked with-one who had hiked on both the Appalachian and the Pacific Crest Trails-told me that while hiking the length of the Kekekabic Trail his feet became so sore and badly blistered that he developed a case of blood poisoning, in spite of heavy duty hiking boots. So don't underrate this trail.

Not everyone who hikes this trail goes the full distance. In addition to day hikers, many backpackers only walk in a few miles to a favorite campsite where they may stay overnight or longer.

I have seen some strange sights while on this trail, including a Twin Cities family that was day hiking on the west end of the trail while shod in shower clogs. It was a good thing that they were not planning to walk very far. Those sharp angular rocks that protrude from the trail's tread can be murder on unprotected toes.

The activity of modern man on the Kekekabic Trail started on the east end of the trail, when Henery Mayhew, a Grand Marais bussinessman, discovered iron ore formations west of Gunflint Lake in the 1880's. In 1886 a group of Grand Marais residents formed the Gunflint Lake Iron Company. Stock was sold and a railroad, the Port Arthur, Duluth, and Western Railroad, was constructed from Port Arther, Ontario (now part of Thunder Bay) to a point just north of the Kekekabic Trail parking lot.

Exploratory operations began in 1892. Several pits were dug, and you will walk pass these on the first mile of the Kekekabic Trail. Two shafts, one 75 feet deep and another dug to 105 feet, were sunk on the north side of Mine (Akeley) Lake. These pits are now marked with Forest Service signs.

The mining area was called Paulson's Mine after its chief promoter. The mining camp was named Paulson's Camp. Later the name of the camp was changed to Gunflint City. All of this came to nothing, as the iron ore was of very poor quality and very little was ever mined. In 1893 the project was abandoned. The railroad was cut back to the Canadian Border and was put to work transporting forest products to Port Arthur. After the collapse of the enterprise, many people said that the whole thing was only a promotion to sell stock.

Soon after the demise of the Gunflint Lake Iron Company a survey line was marked from Paulson's Mine to Ely for a projected railroad. In the 1920's this line was resurveyed for a road. Neither the railroad nor the road was ever started. Later the survey line was relocated as a trail that was used by Minnesota State forestry crews to check on area logging operations.

In 1936, the area became part of the Superior National Forest. The primitive trail was maintained to service the Kekekabic fire tower and guard station on Kekekabic Lake. The trail was a "way" trail for fire protection and forest administration. There was only minimal work on the tread and clearing within the corridor. When the trail was completed in 1938 there was no thought that this "utility path" had any recreational value. One of the first recreational hikers on the Kek was a man who walked in to the tower lugging two full suitcases. Think about that the next time you feel the weight of your backpack.

Although the fire tower was in use until 1956, after the mid 1940's it was serviced by aircraft instead of by the trail. Lacking maintenance by Forest Service crews and use by recreationalists, the trail's condition soon deteriorated.

In August 1949, a group of Senior Scouts of the Lake Superior Council, working under the direction of Council Executive Harry E. Bartelt, cleared out 6.4 miles of the trail from Fay Lake to the Agamok Lake Portage. Whitney Evens, trail boss and scribe for the scout crew, wrote a descripion of the Kekekabic Trail that is applicable today:

> "The Kekekabic Trail is one of the toughest, meanest rabbit tracks in North America. The trail struggles its way through swamps, around cliffs, up the sides of bluffs and across rocky ridges. It is choked with nightmarish patches of clinging brush. It is blocked with tangles of windfalls and standing timber. It is pressed, in places, on all sides by outcroppings of rock; sometimes it snakes its way over old river beds, slippery, rocky and treacherous. In other areas it is a peaceful path loping through open stands of timber with a soft mossy carpet underfoot. Its the kind of a trail that would break the heart of a man who didn't have what it takes to go into the wilderness and try to 'smooth it.' "

Do not expect to be able to walk very fast on this trail. There are many sharp, angular rocks and exposed tree roots, making it necessary to watch where you put your feet. This makes walking slow and tedious. Under these conditions it is impossible to maintain one's stride. In addition, there are always fallen trees and wet places that require time to negotiate.

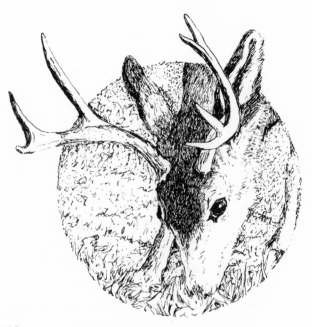

The Trail

Going east to west on the Kekekabic Trail from the Gunflint Trail parking lot, the trail heads up a ridge. After a half mile there is a branch trail to the right that leads to the Gunflint fire tower site. The tower is now used as a radio tower.

Continuing west the trail enters into a narrow valley containing a fast little stream and several small ponds. This part of the trail was once the wagon road to the Paulson's Camp mine at 40-acre Mine Lake, which is the first large body of water you will pass on the trail. After passing several more unnamed ponds, the Boundary Waters Canoe Area marker is reached. Be sure to have a Boundary Waters Canoe Area permit on you and follow the regulations.

A short distance beyond the marker, the trail reaches Bingshick Lake, five miles from the Gunflint parking lot. Near the portage trail between Bingshick Lake and Honker Lake is a campsite. Bingshick Lake is 45-acres in area and has a 1.5-mile shoreline. The lake is supposed to have northern pike and lake trout.

Going west around the north shore of Bingshick Lake the trail crosses the marshy portage between Bingshick and Glee Lakes. The trail is rough and rocky with several hills to go up and down before reaching the Glee Lake-to-Fay Lake portage. Glee Lake has 35-acres with 2 miles of shoreline. Fay Lake is about the same size.

From here it is a short distance of rough walking to the Chub River crossing. On the other side of the river the trail climbs westward to the south side of War Club Lake. There are several places to set up a tent here and the lake offers northern pike fishing.

The trail curves around the west shore of 29-acre War Club Lake, recrosses the Chub River, and parallels it in a western direction along a ridge before dropping down into a valley. There is a crossing of a stream that flows south from Seahorse Lake to an unnamed lake. From here the trail ascends a ridge and passes through an black spruce forest next to the shoreline of Howard Lake.

At this point you are about 10 miles from the Gunflint Trail parking lot.

Howard Lake is a 163-acre lake with a four mile shoreline. There is good fishing for northern pike and lake trout here. A small campsite on the shore is accessible from the trail. The lake is on a main canoe route and you may see canoeists. It is named after the Howard brothers who prospected for the Paulson Mine.

From Howard Lake the trail crosses a stream and climbs a steep hill, and then descends to a low area and crosses another stream.

It is a short walk to a narrow bay of Gabimichigami Lake. The Kekekabic Trail used to follow the shoreline of this large 1,236-acre lake to the outlet of Agomak Lake. There the hiker had to cross a fairly wide river that could be dangerous during a high water period. Now the trail turns right and moves uphill for a mile or more before dropping to a level course and edging around an open marsh area. A quarter of a mile later the trail turns southward and crosses a small stream near a pond. Then the trail goes through the woods a short distance to the Agamok Bridge.

This bridge spans a tumbling, roaring river between Agamok and Mueller. The north-south Mueller Lake-to-Agamok Lake portage is a few yards to the west of the bridge. Mueller Lake is a 30-acre lake with 1.5 miles of shoreline. Agamok Lake is a 105-acre lake with 3.5 miles of shoreline.

The Kekekabic Trail crosses the portage trail and climbs uphill in a southern direction. After a series of ups and downs over hills the trail rejoins the old route of the Kekekabic Trail. From this point the trail continues to be very hilly and rocky. After about a mile it passes the narrow south arm of 12-acre Buswah Lake. This part of the trail can be very muddy. A mile further on, the trail passes Loki Lake, a 33-acre lake with a mile of shoreline. The next lake, a quarter of a mile past Loki, is nameless, with a huge beaver dam at one end. It is a good place to set up camp and watch beavers at work. From this lake it is an uphill grind, with plenty of rocks and windfalls, to the former site of the Kekekabic fire tower. The tower was removed in 1979. Past the tower site it is about three more miles of rocky up and down hiking to the Strup Lake-to-Kekekabic Lake Portage. There is a good place to camp on the Strup Lake end of the portage. Although it is a portage trail there is usually not much traffic.

Strup Lake is a 58-acre Lake with 2.5 miles of shoreline. Kekekabic Lake is a 1,620-acre Lake with more than 18 miles of shoreline. Both Lakes have smallmouth bass and lake trout. Kekekabic Lake is one of the few lakes in the area where it is possible to catch lake trout near the surface in mid-summer.

There is very little grade on the trail for the next five miles from here to the Thomas Lake portage. The first half mile is through a black spruce swamp and then past a small unnamed body of water where there is a campsite to the left of the trail. Further on after a mile and a half of good walking the trail touches the edge of a beaver pond. A mile later there is a large beaver pond with a dam that forms a long bridge for the trail. Both of these beaver ponds are excellent places to observe beaver activity.

It is two easy miles from here to the Thomas Lake-to-Hatchet Lake Portage. The river at this portage has a bridge across it. The trail continues in a southwestern direction and crosses two small streams. The next body of water on the trail is a large beaver pond. An old beaver trapper's campsite is on the shore of this pond. It is an excellent place to camp and listen to the beaver's nighttime work. A long beaver dam forms a long bridge for the trail. It is a half-a-mile to where the trail passes between two small Lakes: 49-acre Moiyaka Lake on the north and 22-acre Medas Lake on the south. Both of these two lakes offer good campsites.

The remaining 10 miles of the Kekekabic Trail are more or less uneventful up and down hill walking with small stream crossings. The trail sticks to a southwest course until it passes the Snowbank Lake Trail intersections. At the point east of the junction with the Snowbank Lake Trail on the southeast corner of Parent Lake, a spur trail leaves the Kekekabic trail to the left. This trail passes by 52-acre Becoosin and 59-acre Benezie Lakes before rejoining the Kek just south of Parent Lake. There are campsites on both of these small lakes.

Heading west, the remaining distance goes up and down hills through an old logging area and ends at the Fernberg Road less than a mile north of the Lake One Landing.

In the 1960's and 70's the Superior National Forest, in response to growing public interest in backpacking, cleared out the entire trail, rerouted the path around some wet areas, and developed several loop trails.

Lately, however, the Kekekabic Trail has fallen on hard times. Thanks in part to Forest Service budget cuts, and in part to short sighted decisions made by some Superior National Forest staff members, maintenance of the Kekekabic trail ended. This was followed by the removal of the Kekekabic Trail from Forest Service maps and informational material. Trailhead signs on the Gunflint Trail and Fernberg Road were taken down. Forest Service information personnel were instructed by their superiors to refer those recreationists who expressed interest in hiking the Kekekabic Trail to other foot trails.

It appeared to many, including this writer, that the Superior National Forest was very determined to stop the use of the Kekekabic Trail by hikers. The Kek almost passed into history.

In order to save the Kekekabic Trail, Bruce Mellor of Little Falls, Minnesota has formed *The Friends of the Kekekabic trail*. His efforts have included the circulation of petitions in support of the trail as well as promotion of the use of volunteer work crews to do maintenance work on the trail.

The petitions signed by many, including the Minnesota governor, show strong public support for The Friends of the Kekekabic Trail.

At the present time both ends of the trail are in good shape, but the center section should only be hiked by experienced hikers until the entire trail can be maintained.

This would be a shame to the Superior National Forest and a loss to everyone to abandon the Kekekabic Trail at a time of growing interest in backpacking. Minnesota hikers are forced to go out of state find true wilderness trails while a great trail like the Kek is allowed to go back to nature. As Bruce Mellor, spokesperson for the Friends of the Kekekabic Trail writes:

"Besides being a mere foot path, the Kek has exceptional education and scenic values as it traverses a maze of virgin timber types and ecological zones. The trail is also located for most of its length along a corridor of geological contacts which makes the Kek a one of a kind access to viewing the geological history of the BWCA."

If you want to help preserve the Kekekabic Trail for hiking, contact:
Bruce Mellor
Friends of the Kekekabic Trail
312-1/2 SE Third Street
Little Falls, MN 56345

Snowbank Lake and Old Pines Trails

These two trails are part of the western end of the Kekekabic Trail. The trailhead for both trails is at the Kekekabic Trail parking lot, which is a half a mile from the eastern end of the Fernberg Road (County Road 18), 26 miles east of Ely. On the official state highway map the grid location is O-6.

A BWCA permit is required to hike these trails.

The Snowbank Lake Trail is a semi-loop trail around 4,819-acre Snowbank Lake. The two ends of the trail are two miles apart. It is the hope of this writer that this trail will be made into a loop. Starting from the parking lot, the Snowbank Lake Trail follows the route of the Kekekabic Trail. At a point south of 412-acre Parent Lake, a side trail branches off to the right (south). This is a short half-loop trail that gives the hiker access to Becoosin and Benezie

Lakes. There are campsites on both lakes. The trail returns to the Kekekabic Trail east of the Snowbank Trail junction on the southeast corner of Parent Lake. From this point the Snowbank Lake Trail leaves the Kekekabic Trail in a northeast direction along an open ridge. About halfway up the east side of the Lake there is a campsite to the left of the trail.

Past this point the trail enters a stand of jack pine near a bog that was once a lake.

The trail returns to the northwest corner of Parent Lake. Past the lake the direction is northeast toward the portage trail between Parent and Disappointment Lakes. After crossing the portage trail near 950-acre Disappointment Lake, the Snowbank Lake Trail follows the west shore of the lake. A long, narrow channel is formed between the lakeshore and an island, giving the channel the appearance of a wide, deep river.

Near the end of this channel the trail turns northward and away from the lake. Passing a campsite to the left, the trail ascends to a rocky viewpoint high on a ridge.

From the ridge, the trail moves through open groves of jack pine, past Birdseye Lake on the right (east). Beyond Birdseye Lake the northbound trail touches the northeast corner of Snowbank Lake. A lakeside campsite is located to the left. Past this point, the Old Pines Trail comes in from the right (southeast) to join with the Snowbank Lake Trail. The Old Pines Trail will be described later in this section.

From here the Snowbank Lake Trail continues northward. After a stream crossing there is a turn to the left (west), which puts the trail on an open and rocky ridge. Near the point where the trail starts to descend there is a campsite on the left. Another lakeside campsite is located near the bottom of the ridge.

Past the campsite there is an ascent up a ridge with spectacular views in several directions. Down from the ridge the trail's direction is first west through hills and dales before turning northward. This is followed by a swing to the southwest past the northwest shore of 41-acre Grub Lake. About halfway past the lake there is a campsite on the right side of the trail. Continuing to the southwest, the trail returns to Snowbank Lake near a campsite. A short distance along the shore there is another lakeside campsite on a stream that flows in from Wooden Leg Lake.

Northwestward, the trail goes up a ridge and then circles around the north side of 26-acre Wooden Leg Lake. Past the lake there is a turn to the west and up a ridge with a view to the northwest. From a high point there is a turn to the southwest along the northwest shores of Snowbank Lake. Half a mile along the lake is a lakefront campsite. A quarter of a mile farther on is a ledge top campsite to the right of the trail.

Beyond this campsite is an ascent to a overlook above the lake. From the high point the trail drops to a campsite to the right of the trail. This is the last campsite on the Snowbank Lake Trail. Shortly afterward it's back up a ridge to enjoy another vista. Near the southeast corner of Snowbank Lake, the trail crosses the Snowbank Lake-to-Flash Lake portage. From here on in the Snowbank Lake Trail goes up and down through forested hills to the Snowbank Lake Road. At the road, turn right (southwest) and continue for a mile and a half to the paved Fernberg Road. Once on the Fernberg Road take a left and walk three-quarters of a mile to the Kekekabic Trail parking lot.

Old Pines Trail

This a loop trail off the old Kekekabic Trail, with a connection to the Snowbank Lake Trail just described. From the same parking lot on the Fernberg Road follow the Kekekabic Trail eastward. At a place south of the east end of Disappointment Lake there is a trail coming in from the north. This trail is the west side of the Old Pines Trail loop. More on this part of the Old Pines Trail later.

Walk east, on the bottom (south) side of the Old Pines Loop. A mile farther on, the trail passes the north shore of 19-acre Drumstick Lake, where there is a campsite built on the former location of a 1900s logging camp.

Heading northeast past Drumstick Lake the trail soon starts to swing southward through a forest of paper birch. After a stream crossing on an old beaver dam, the trail enters a stand of large, mature white pine, for which the Old Pines Trail was named. The trail makes several bends around the pines, allowing for more time to walk among these huge, old trees.

From the Old Pine groves the trail's course is to the east and then north through areas of open pine forest, to pass by the eastern shores of 22-acre Medas and 49-acre Moiya lakes. Both of these small lakes have a campsite. The Medas Lake campsite is on a point jutting out from the northeast shore. The Moiya Lake campsite is on its south shore, west of a small stream between the two lakes.

Moving north past the two lakes a trail branches off the Old Pines Trail heading east. This is the famous Kekekabic Trail, which ends at the Gunflint Trail (County Road 12) at a point 57 miles northeast of Grand Marais.

The Old Pines Trail direction turns to the west at the south shore of 228-acre Alworth Lake. A spur trail off to the right leads to a lakeshore campsite. Farther west a stream is crossed on a beaver dam.

From this point on, the trail covers hills and swamps as well as open areas of bare rock, before joining a trail junction. At this junction a turn to the left (south) will put the hiker on the previously mentioned west side of the Old Pines Trail. This arm of the Old Pines Trail runs southeast past the east side of Disappointment Lake, to rejoin the Kekekabic Trail a short distance west of the Drumstick Lake campsite.

From this same junction, a turn to the right (north) takes you over pine forested ridges and between Ahsub and Disappointment Lakes. There are campsites on both lakes. A portage trail between the two lakes is crossed. West of the portage there is spur trail to the right (north) to another campsite on the west side of 70-acre Ahsub Lake.

This trail continues eastward to form a junction with the Snowbank Lake Trail near the northeast shore of Snowbank Lake.

For maps and other information about Kawishiwi Ranger District Trails contact:
Superior National Forest
Kawishiwi Ranger District
118 S. 4th Ave. E.
Ely, MN 55731
(218) 365-6185P

It is always a good idea to stop at the Forest Service Voyageur Visitor Center in Ely to check on current trail conditions before starting out on a hike.

LaCroix Ranger District

Astrid Trails

This trail system is next to the Lake Jeanette Campground, on the Echo Trail (County Road 116) about 38 miles northwest of Ely. On the official state highway map its grid location is M-5.

A BWCA permit is not required for this trail system.

There are about six miles of trail, which can be day hiked or backpacked. Day hikers may elect to camp at the Lake Jeanette Campground. For backpackers there are several wilderness camp-sites (fire grates, box latrines) at several lakes along the trail.

The Astrid Trail crosses the Echo Trail a half a mile from the Lake Jeanette Campground. Hikers must be very careful crossing the road, as drivers may be unaware of the trail crossing.

After crossing the road, the trail passes westward through a spruce bog on the Lake Jeanette-to-Nigh Lake portage trail. Before reaching Nigh Lake the hiking trail branches to the left off of the portage trail. From here there are a series of switchbacks up a ridge to enter the longer of the two loops that make up most of the Astrid Trails system. There are some outstanding views of the cliffs and lakes from the ridge.

Going west on the north side of the loop, the trail passes the junction with the smaller northern loop. More on this loop later. At the second junction, the trail to the south follows the east shoreline of 114-acre Astrid Lake to a wilderness campsite. The trail then turns southeast. Before turning northeast, a spur trail leaves the loop's southwest corner for the south shore of Astrid Lake. On the west side of the lake the trail joins the Astrid Lake-to-Maude Lake port-age trail. This portage trail crosses County Road 200 at its midpoint.

Back at the main loop, the trail turns back to the northwest, go-ing up and down across ridgelines to the point where the loop was entered.

The shorter northern loop heads up to the portage trail between Nigh and Pauline lakes. At the Pauline Lake end of the portage trail the loop trail follows the southern shore of the lake past a spur trail, then branches west to a lakeside wilderness campsite. Pauline Lake is a 60-acre Lake.

Among some of the features of the northern loop are some huge boulders that are said to be the largest in the area, and several rather impressive stands of old growth red and white pine. Farther south there is a junction with the main loop.

Big Moose Trail

This three mile trail is reached by Forest Road 464, about two miles south of the Echo Trail forest Road 116, 27 miles northwest of Ely. The trail begins at the parking area and goes south through two-and-a-half miles of lowland forest. It then changes direction to the southwest and goes up and down hills for the remaining one-half mile to reach 1,116-acre Big Moose Lake. Because the last part of this trail is within the BWCA a travel permit is required.

It is a well-marked trail, but because it goes across low, boggy land, it is best used in late summer or fall when the soil is in drier condition. Because of its length, it can be hiked in a day, and if the fish are biting, you can catch walleyes, pike, and other good eating fish. (During the winter, snowmobiling is allowed; use Fisher map No. 112.)

Herriman Lake Trail

The Herriman Lake Trail system is one-and-a-half miles south of the town of Crane Lake on County road 424. On the official state highway map its grid location is L-5.

There is off-the-road parking on the west side of the road. From the parking lot the trail crosses the road and heads east. A mile into the forest there is a picnic site at the Echo River bridge. The Echo Trail is named after this river. The picnic site is for day use only, as camping is not allowed. Three Boundary Waters Canoe Area type campsites are in the trail system.

From the bridge, the main trail is to the east. After passing by Knute Lake to the north the trail ends near a campsite on 550-acre Little Vermillion Lake. This long, narrow lake forms part of the international boundary between the United States and Canada. During the days of the Northwest Company fur trade, Little Vermillion Lake was on the main lake and river route from Grand Portage to the Canadian Northwest.

There are several loop trails that branch off from this trail. One is a short loop that leaves the main trail near Kunte Lake and heads south past a remote campsite on the 13-acre lake. Past the lake the trail turns east to rejoin the main trail. This loop trail is connected to another loop trail that runs southward to circle an area of hills before returning north to tie back into the main trail. At the south side of this last loop another trail drops in a southern direction to go up a steep ridge before heading west to tie into the Echo River Trail loop. On the way to the Echo River there are some great views of Herriman Lake to the north of the trail.

In the opinion of many who have hiked the Herriman Lake Trail system, the Echo River Trail loop is the most scenic part of the system. The trail starts at the bridge and follows the Echo River south. The path is quite level until it starts uphill to turn around on the ridgtop loop. At the loop there are several overlooks with views of the Echo River Valley.

The Dovre Lake loop is the only trail loop north of the main trail. It connects to the main trail just north of Knute Lake. It is an up-and-down ridgeline trail that provides good exercise on the way to 110-acre Dovre Lake. From a ridge overlooking Dovre Lake there is a picture postcard view of the landscape. A spur trail leads to a remote lakeshore BWCA campsite. The west side of this loop turns south back into the main trail a third of a mile east of the Echo River bridge.

The 14 miles of trails in the Herriman Lake Trail system are good for a weekend or more of excellent day hiking or backpacking. For those day hikers who do not want to camp, there are several resorts in the Crane Lake area a mile and a half north of the trail's parking lot on County Road 424.

Because more than half of the Herriman Lake Trail system is within the BWCA, a travel permit is required to hike these trails.

Norway Trail

The Norway Trail starts 17 mile southeast of Buyck, a small town on the west end of the Echo Trail. It is an eight mile, north-south trail from the Echo Trail to the North Arm of Trout Lake. It was constructed during the 1930's to serve the Norway Firetower.

Because only the last half of this trail is within the boundary Waters Canoe Area, a travel permit is required. Most of the trail has been used by snowmobiliers. As a result of this winter use, the trail is cleared of brush, well marked, and easy to follow.

The trail starts on the south side of the Echo Trail. There is no place to park a vehicle off the road at this trailhead. Vehicles can be parked at the Jeanette Lake Campground, a mile to the west.

There is also a drive-in parking place at a side road about halfway between the campground and the trail. The parking place is apparently used by snowmachine operators. The snowmobilers use an unimproved forest road from here to enter the Norway Trail.

The trailhead is marked with a sign. The trail takes off through the usual second growth of mixed broadleaf and needle. The forest was logged off before the 1940's, however, there are still small stands of large red and white pine scattered along the path.

About one-fifth of a mile from the road the trail is crossed by the unimproved road from the snowmobilier's parking lot. A half mile farther on another unimproved road joins from the west.

The trail traverses gently rolling terrain interspersed with patches of black spruce swamp. In some of these patches there are wide areas of swamp that are bridged by planking. The next five miles is up and down hills and thorugh the swamps, then the trail branches off to the west. This is a snowmobile trail to Orinjack Lake. A half-mile past this snowmobile trail there is a foot trail going east to the site of the Norway firetower a little farther ahead. From this point on the Norway Trail, it is only a mile-and-a-half to the trail's end at the North Arm of Trout Lake.

The last one-half mile of the trail is within the BWCA, therefore, if you camp on the North Arm, you have to have a travel permit and follow BWCA regulations.

This trail is really not in very good condition to hike at the present time due to the poor condition of the swamp crossings. No real hiker minds going through an occasional mud hole or creek, but this amount of slogging is almost too much.

The Norway Trail could be more interesting and useful for outdoor recreation if it were looped to reach Orinjack, Picket, Maude, and Nigh Lakes. This would make a trail of 25 miles or so that would begin and end at the same place.

The nearest Forest Service Campground is at Jeanette Lake, about one mile west of the trailhead. (Use Fisher map No. 111 for this trail.)

Sioux-Hustler Trail

The Sioux-Hustler is a trail for the experienced backpacker who is looking for a challenge. This is definitely not the trail for a first backpacking experience.

It is a hard trail to hike: brushy, poorly marked and blocked by fallen timber. The backpacker often has to spend time looking for the trail. In addition, there are many streams and swampy areas. None of these are bridged, so they have to be waded.

This trail is now a loop. Before, when it was a semiloop trail, a hiker would end up seven miles from the starting point. Now, thanks to the staff of the LaCroix Ranger District, hikers and skiers can make the loop from the Meander Lake picnic site, where there is a parking lot and primitive campsites.

Meander Lake is off the Echo Trail (County Road 116) about 45 miles northwest of Ely. On the official state highway map its grid location is M-6.

Starting from the Meander Lake trailhead, the trail heads northwest to the Sioux river and parallels its east bank for half a mile. The path then turns north for the next two miles, running through fairly hilly country to the portage trail between Lower Pauness and Shell Lakes. From here it is less than a mile to Devil's Cascade, a series of waterfalls of the Little Indian Sioux River. There is a small Forest Service campsite here with table and fireplace. Because the river is a popular canoe route, it is possible that a canoe party will be camped there.

After another mile through gentle hills, the trail enters the land of brush and mush (swamp). It is about two-and-a-half miles of wet-dry-wet walking to the Loon Lake to Heritage Lake portage. This is a rough stretch of trail to backpack, but the wildlife seem to like it, judging from the amount of tracks that are always visible.

The next half-mile takes you to Heritage Creek. As with all streams on this trail, one must wade. As you wade in cold water above your knees, remind yourself of the many hikers who would be sharing trail if it were not for the barriers such as these unbridged streams and swamps. Enjoy your solitude!

From Heritage Creek, it is one mile or so of slightly improved walking to the west end of Pageant Lake, where beavers always seem to be putting on a show. This 48-acre lake has a small Forest Service campsite for hikers. When the weather is fair and the bugs are not too active, this is a good place to relax and rest from your rigors.

From Pageant Lake the trail turns southwest. After a half-mile, it crosses Pageant Creek. The trail then passes between Range Line lake on the south and an unnamed lake on the north. Range Line Lake is a 106-acre lake, with three miles of shoreline. The northeast corner looks like a good place to cast for northerns and walleyes.

The next two miles of trail traverse more lowland forest, then comes four miles of fairly good hiking. Two miles farther on, the trail reaches the east arm of Hustler Lake. This 272-acre lake has walleyes and northerns.

Just south of a creek coming in from Weeny Lake, a portage trail going east to Oyster Lake crosses the Sioux-Hustler Trail. Judging from tracks seen on the soft earth of the portage, both deer and moose like to use this trail. From here the direction of the trail turns from southeast to south. It is another mile to the northeast arm of Emerald Lake, which covers 57-acres and has two miles of shoreline. The Forest Service campsite on this Emerald Lake is the last one on the east side of the trail. There are places near the camp-site where you can fish.

The trail goes up and down hills for a mile until it drops to cross Shohola Creek, another experience in wading. After the creek crossing there is another mile of hilly hiking to an area of swamp that is the northern boundary of the Little Indian Sioux Fire of 1971. In that year, between May 14 and 19, one of the hottest fires in the Superior National Firest in more than 30 years, consumed 15,000-acres of forest land. It took 500 firefighters, a lot of machin-ery, and some rain to bring this fire under control.

The remaining four miles of the trail go over the low hills and through the swamps of the burned area. The trail ends at a parking lot one-quarter mile from the Meander Lake Picnic Area.

Sioux-Hustler Trail is within the BWCA, and subject to those regulations. (Use Fisher map No. 107 for this trail.)

A recent change in the Sioux-Hustler has been the addition of a cutoff trail that makes for a shorter loop trek. With this new nine-mile section of trail there are now a total of 35 miles of trail in the Sioux-Hustler Trail system. The new shorter loop, called the Shell Lake Loop, cuts the round-trip distance from Meander Lake down to about 16 miles. However, bear in mind that the north side of the new loop is in good part up and down along ridgelines. For many hikers this rough topography makes the Shell Lake Loop too long for a day hike. So plan for at least one night of camping on the loop.

while the old 26-mile-long Sioux-Hustler Trail may be too long for a weekend backpacking trip, the 16-mile-long Shell Lake Loop should be closer to the ideal weekend trip for the average backpacker.

Going clockwise from the Meander Lake starting point, the new trail section fo the Shell Lake Loop branches off from the old trail at a point north of the Lower Pauness Lake-to-Shell Lake portage, turning right. After that the trail follows a ridgeline in a northeastern direction. Next, the trail edges the north side of 484-acre Shell Lake. From the ridge, the trail drops down to the Shell Lake-to-Heritage Lake portage is in the stream valley between the two lakes. The trail is on this portage for about 50 feet before it cuts off it by going southeast, then continues along a ridge passing the northeast shore of Shell Lake. Several high points on the ridgeline offer opportunities for scenic viewing of lakes and hills.

Soon the trail drops down and passes through a narrow gap of land between Shell and Little Shell lakes to a portage trail between the two lakes. After crossing this portage, the trail continued in a southeastern direction, passing around the south side of 13-acre Agawato Lake. From here on the course is due east until there is a junction with the old part of the Sioux-Hustler Trail south of Emerald Lake.

Stuart Lake Trail

The Stuart Lake Trail, formerly called the Lac La Croix Trail, starts off the Echo Trail about 21 miles north of Ely. The trail was built to service a guard station on Lac La Croix. At the present time the trail beyond Stuart Lake is impassable. It is to be hoped that the section of trail between Stuart Lake and Lac La Croix will be renovated.

After the trail leaves the trailhead parking lot it heads north as a two-rut truck trail. After a quarter of a mile it narrows to a one-lane hiking trail. The forest cover is made up of mixed coniferous and deciduous trees. The first four miles were logged in the years between 1940 and 1968. The remainder of the trail passes through virgin forest. The topography is generally low with few hills.

After three miles the trail passes by the west side of Mule Lake. This is a 48-acre lake with 1.2 miles of shoreline. The shoreline on the west side is low and marshy, making it difficult, if not impossible to fish from this side. However, the east side of the lake appears to be high and rocky. So if you could make it round to the east side, you might try to fish this seldom fished lake.

Past Mule Lake the trail continues north for a mile or so. It then turns northeast for 2.5 miles, going around an area of wetland before crossing the Stuart River. This is an easy crossing and with any luck you will not get your feet wet. A short distance further on, the trail reaches the east shore of Stuart Lake and follows the shoreline until it corsses the Stuart Lake-to-Nibin Lake portage.

The westbound arm of this crossroad ends at a camping area on the shore of Stuart Lake.

Stuart Lake is a beautiful 735-acre lake with 8.7 miles of shoreline. It has populations of walleyes, northern pike, and lake trout. Nibin Lake on the other end of the portage trail is a 38-acre lake with a mile of shoreline. The fishing potential is unknown. Because this trail is partly in the BWCA, a permit is required.

For a map and further information on La Croix Ranger District Trails contact:

Superior National Forest
La Croix Ranger District
P.O. Box 1085
Cook, MN 55723
(218) 555-5251

Tofte Ranger District

Oberg Mountain Loop Trail

This outstanding, scenic 2.25-mile-long trail is located about 5 miles northeast of Tofte, off of North Shore Highway 61. On the official state highway map its grid location is O-7.

After passing the Ray Berglund State Scenic Memorial Wayside turn left (west) onto Forest Road 336 (Onion River Road). From the highway it is 2.2 miles to the trail's parking lot. From the parking lot the trail heads east, crosses Forest Road 336, and runs through a level area of forest towards Oberg Mountain. The trail takes several switchbacks in a gradual ascent up Oberg Mountain that does not require a great deal of effort.

There are several benches along this trail section to take a restful view. When walking this short trail there is no reason to hurry, so take enough time to enjoy the sights.

Near the summit, the trail joins the loop that circles the top of Oberg Mountain. Most hikers take the turn to the right, taking the loop in a counterclockwise direction. There are nine scenic overviews along this loop, with some great views of Lake Superior and the forested hills and wetlands.

It is very difficult to see any evidence of human activity from the top of Oberg Mountain. Even North Shore Highway 61 is out of sight, under the crest of the ridge. So what you see is how the north shore of Lake Superior may have appeared before white settlement. It is almost like going back in a time machine.

In the opinion of many hikers this trail is one of the most scenic North Shore trails.

The trail sometimes passes close to steep cliffs, so there are signs warning parents to keep small children in hand.

The Oberg Mountain Loop Trail has a connection to the Superior Hiking Trail that will eventually extend from Duluth to Canada.

Onion River Trail

This short North Shore trail starts from the Ray Berglund State Scenic Memorial Wayside about four miles northeast of Tofte on the North Shore Drive Highway 61. On the official state highway map its grid location is P-7.

Ray Berglund was a prominent lumberman and conservationist, who did much to help preserve the natural beauty of the North Shore.

As with all such state waysides there is ample parking space, along with picnic facilities. Waysides are day-use sites only, camping is not permitted.

The Onion River Trail starts on a hill on the west side of the parking lot. A small sign points toward the Onion River, named after the wild onion that once grew here. The trail following this wild river is a little more than a half a mile long. However short the trail, walking through groves of old growth white pine, spruce, and fir gives the feeling of what the North Shore of Lake Superior may have looked like before white settlement. Also, the natural beauty of the Onion River in its mad rush towards Lake Superior in a series of wild falls and rapids makes the strenuous uphill hike worth the effort.

Superior Hiking Trail

When completed, this long hiking trail will extend along Minnesota's Lake Superior North Shore, from Duluth to the Canadian border, an estimated distance of 200 miles. Enroute, the trail will pass through two state forests, seven state parks and the Superior National Forest.

The Superior Hiking Trail is unique in that it is a single-use trail, and that use is hiking.

As of now the Superior Hiking Trail has over 100 miles of completed trail. An additional 50 miles of trail will be ready by the end of fiscal year 1989, along with support facilities such as bridges and campsites.

At the present time access points to the trail include: Split Rock Lighthouse State Park, Temperance River State Park, Tettegouche State Park and Superior Forest Road 336 just north of the Ray Berglund Wayside.

It seems only reasonable that a completed Superior Hiking Trail would connect to the Grand Portage Trail, and through it to the Border Route Trail, and the Kekekabic Trail. This would form one long hiking trail from Duluth to the Fernberg Road (Saint Louis County Road 18), 26 miles east of Ely.

Linked together these four trails would form a good part of the North Country Trail through Minnesota. The North Country Trail is a national hiking trail through the northern states, from New York State to North Dakota.

In the meantime, the Superior Hiking Trail Association needs more members to work on building and maintaining the trail. This is an excellent opportunity for individuals and organizations to help develop a world class hiking trail through the Minnesota Arrowhead region.

For maps and further information on the Superior Hiking Trail contact:
Superior Hiking Trail Association
P.O. Box 2157
Tofte, MN 55615
(218) 663-7981

For maps and further information on the Tofte Ranger District trails contact:
Superior National Forest
Tofte Ranger District
Tofte, MN 55615
(218) 663-7981

National Park Service Trails

Grand Portage National Monument

The historic village of Grand Portage lies on the shores of Lake Superior, 157 miles northeast of Duluth on Highway 61. The Indian name for Grand Portage is *Kitchi-Onigan,* which translates into "Big Portage." When you arrive at Grand Portage you will see the stockade and reconstructed buildings of the U.S. Park Service's Grand Portage National Monument. At the Great Hall there are displays of trade goods, and, Indian artifacts, and historical interpretations of the fur trade era.

In the days of the fur trade, between 1770 and 1803, Grand Portage was a very busy place. Every summer, two fleets of canoes would converge on the Grand Portage post. Paddling around Hat Point would come "Pork Eaters" in large 40-foot canoes, transporting cargos of trade goods from Montreal. At about the same time, "Northmen" from the Canadian northwest would be docking their 25-foot canoes loaded with bales of fur at the Pigeon River Post of Fort Charlotte.

At Grand Portage, both groups of voyageurs would exchange cargos and then prepare to return to their home bases. Since both groups had to made a round trip of more than 3,000 miles in less than four months, they could not stay more than a few days at Grand Portage. The "Pork Eaters" returned to Montreal with fur for the markets of Europe, while the "Northmen" transported trade goods back to the northwest to barter for more fur. During their short stay at Grand Portage the two groups camped in segregated areas.

Grand Portage Trail

The nine mile-long Grand Portage Trail starts at the reconstructed stockade near the Lake Superior shoreline. At this point the trail's elevation is a little more than 600 feet above sea level. When the trail reaches the western end at Fort Charlotte on the Pigeon river, it will have gained 700 feet in elevation.

From the stockade area the trail enters the wide valley of Grand Portage Creek and follows it upstream. Three-quarters of a mile later the path crosses Highway 61 and passes through a high gap in the ridgeline.

After a short distance, the trail drops down into the valley of the Popular River, crossing the river on a bridge. From there the trail goes up and down a series of ridges, crossing two small streams before reaching the old North Shore Highway, which is now a county road. This is three miles from the stockade. The path then gently climbs up and through a narrow gap, which is the only pass in a long, rocky ridge.

There is then a turn to the west in order to miss a large area of swamps. This part of the trail is crossed by several streams and it can be very muddy.

About three-quarters of a mile before the trail reaches the Pigeon River, a branch trail turns to the east, to end at the Cascades of the Split Rock Canyon.

The Cascades area is one of the most scenic places in Minnesota. Here, The Pigeon River plunges deep into a zig-zag canyon. From the United States side of this canyon you can look across a narrow falls that marks the international boundary. There is a view of a long diabase ridge on the Canadian side.

Recent history is seen in the remains of the Pigeon River Log and Boom Company that logged the area in the 1920's. Still visible are parts of the dams and sluiceways the company used to transport logs down the Pigeon River.

There are no established camping sites at the Cascades. This area is not part of the Grand Portage National Monument, it is on the Grand Portage Indian Reservation. In the future the Grand Portage Band may develop and maintain a campground here.

From the Cascades, a half-mile-long trail heads west and follows the Pigeon River upstream to meet the end of the main trail at the site of Fort Charlotte. The U.S. Park Service has a campground here with facilities for 20 campers.

In the days of the fur trade Fort Charlotte was a depot for the "Northmen" who carried their furs over the portage to the Grand Portage Post. Later they transported trade goods from Grand Portage back to Fort Charlotte. The fort is said to be named after the wife of King George III of Great Britain who was the reigning sovereign during the American Revolutionary War.

The condition of the Grand Portage Trail depends on the weather and ranges from good to poor. In wet weather, stream crossings and low areas may be very muddy. This can be a tough trail to hike and not everyone makes it to the end.

Mount Josephine Trail

The Mount Josephine Trail is about a mile east of the stockade at Grand Portage National Monument. The mountain was named for the daughter of a Detroit businessman, John Godfrey, who owned the trading post at Grand Marais. She was said to have walked up to the top in 1853. Mount Josephine is a high ridge that forms a peninsula separating Grand Portage Bay from Waus-Wa-Going Bay. *Waus-Wa-Going* is Ojibway for "Fishing by Torchlight," because the Indians used to spear fish from canoes in the bay with the aid of birch bark torches.

Although the trail is less than two miles in length, the fact that it is mostly uphill makes it a strenuous hike. It is best to take this trail slowly and enjoy the views, which are some of the most spectacular in Minnesota. Be sure to have your camera and canteen with you.

Mount Rose Trail

The Mount Rose Trail is a self-guided nature trail that starts near the Grand Portage stockade and goes up to the top of Mount Rose, 500 feet above the waters of Lake Superior. From this vantage point one has a remarkable view of the reconstructed fur trading post, Grand Portage Bay, and the distant Isle Royale National Park. The Mount Rose Trail is part of the National Monument and is a well-developed, blacktopped trail, complete with steps, benches, and interpretive signs that explain the visible landmarks. The trail was undoubtedly named for the wild roses you see here.

For nearby accommodations there is a campground in Grand Portage. There is also the Grand Portage Lodge, which has a fine restaurant.

or further information contact:
Superintendent
Grand Portage National Monument
Box 666, Grand Marais, MN 55604
(218) 387-2788

Isle Royale National Park

Today I have grown taller from walking with the trees.

Karle Wilson (Mrs. Thomas Ellis Baker)

Although politically a part of the state of Michigan, Isle Royale is more closely tied in its geology, geography, biology, and even its sociology, with the Minnesota Arrowhead country. That is why we have included Isle Royale and its trails in this book.

Isle Royale is the largest island in Lake Superior. The southwestern tip of Isle Royale lies 18 miles from the Minnesota shore at Grand Portage. The mainland Indians called Isle Royale "the floating island" and undoubtedly had a very interesting explanation of its origin.

The geologists' explanation is that the island is the result of successive flows of lava interbedded with sandstone and conglomerates of the Kewenawan series of the pre-Cambrian Era. A series of geologic upheavals resulted in the lava flows being pushed upward to form long parallel ridges, which run in a northeast-southwest direction.

Over thousands of years, the softer rock surrounding these flows eroded away, exposing the hard lava ridges and valleys that now form Isle Royale. The northwest facing slope of these ridges is very steep, while the southeastern slope is more gradual. The map of Lake Superior shows that the island's long axis parallels Minnesota's North Shore as well as the Keweenaw Peninsula of Michigan, 50 miles to the southeast.

Because of its isolation, Isle Royale has long been considered an excellent natural laboratory. In fact, the island has been the site of many years of intensive study of the preditor-prey relationship between moose and wolf populations there. Isle Royale is quite famous for both its moose herds and its two wolf packs.

But the moose and wolf are relatively recent arrivals on Isle Royale. It is speculated that they probably crossed over from the mainland on ice bridges formed during particularly severe winters. The moose arrived sometime during the early part of this century, and the wolf, in the late 1940's.

The woodland caribou was at one time the dominant deer of the island, but they disappeared by about 1925. There are other species of mammals that inhabit the mainland that have never been found on Isle Royale. These include the black bear, racoon, bobcat, skunk, woodchuck, and porcupine. However, red fox, snowshoe hare, beaver, and red squirrel are quite prevalent on the island.

Birch, pine, aspen, cedar, fir, spruce, and in some areas, sugar maple, are the common trees of Isle Royale.

One hundred and ninety-seven species of birds, both resident and migrant, have been observed on the island. Frequently sees birds are the loon, herring gull, black duck, heron, blue jays, canada jays, woodpeckers, and occasionally the sharptailed grouse. Also quite common are the goldeneye, raven, sandpiper, crow, and many small songbirds. Among the large, preditor birds found on Isle Royale are the osprey, bald eagle, and some species of hawk.

Accessible only by boat or plane, and with its interior open only to foot travel, Isle Royale National Park, offers 200 square miles of wilderness beauty and one of the most unique backpacking experiences in the country.

Hiking the island's 120 miles of trails is becoming increasingly more popular every year, and park managers report that Isle Royale is rapidly approaching its maximum use limit. By its relative inaccessibility from major cities, however, Isle Royale is protected from overuse. Water access to the island is limited. The same holds true for air transportation, and this is even further restricted by the rather high cost. Thus, it would seem that Isle Royale will remain as near to its natural state as possible.

Surprisingly enough, this remote island has been subjected to the influence of humans for more than 4,500 years. Prehistoric Indians mined Isle Royale's deposits of pure copper for more than 1,500 years. Although this was by no means a highly organized mining effort, over 1,000 pits were dug by these early miners.

The copper was fashioned into knives, spearheads, and other utilitarian objects, as well as ornaments. It is reported that artifacts fashioned from Isle Royale copper have been discovered as far away as New England and Mexico.

Knowledge of the copper deposits persisted through Indian legend and eventually reached white explorers. In fact, it was probably the stories of a copper rich island that prompted exploration of western Lake Superior. French maps of the lake, made during the last half of the 17th century, show the island with varying degrees of accuracy giving it the name Isle Minong.

Following the Revolutionary War, in the Treaty of Paris signed in 1783, Benjamin Franklin, managed to have the international boundary drawn through the center of Lake Superior and north of Isle Royale to Pigeon Point. Thus, Britain ceded what is now the Minnesota shore, plus Isle Royale, to the fledgling United States. It was probably because of the suspected mineral wealth of the island that Franklin was so persistent in these terms.

Michigan was the first of the Lake Superior territories to be admitted to the Union, and so Isle Royale was given to that state in 1837. A treaty signed by Chippewa in 1843 relinquished Indian claims to the island. Before 1843, there had only been some temporary white settlement of Isle Royale, chiefly by seasonal fishermen. Thus, the treaty opened the island to full-scale prospecting.

By 1847, a dozen mining companies had been established on Isle Royale, and a peak population of 120 people stayed there that summer. This was the first of three short-lived boom periods for mining on Isle Royale. The miners found that copper ore could not be economically extracted, and by 1892 mining was finished.

Commercial fishing had was established as early as 1837, when the American Fur Company established seasonal fishing stations on Isle Royale. Even though the company ceased operations in 1841, fishermen remained on the island. In fact, commercial fishing has provided the longest continuous economic activity conducted on Isle Royale, and still continues today, although barely a remnant of earlier days.

The 50-year history of commercial copper mining on Isle Royale has left many abandoned mine sites. But the island was never completely abandoned. During a mining lull in the 1860's, Isle Royale began to take on, very gradually, its most successful enterprise, tourism.

By the time the first flurry of mining activity died down around 1855, Isle Royale had already gained a reputation as a health resort. During the 1860's and 1870's, excursion steamers were bringing people to Isle Royale and writers of the period were singing the praises of this natural paradise. Isle Royale became a well-known haven for hay-fever sufferers and by the turn of the century, large resorts were established on the island.

The growth of the tourism and resort industry benefited the island's commercial fishermen as well. Visitors and summer residents owning cottages on the island provided an additional outlet for fresh and smoked fish, however, the mainland markets, principally in Duluth, received the bulk of the commercial catch. The fishing families, mainly Norwegians, lived for the most part on the Minnesota shore and came to the island in early spring, staying until late in the fall. Occasionally a few families would winter over on the island. Likewise, during the 1920's and 30's, there was a permanent fisherman's settlement at Chippewa Harbor, complete with schoolhouse.

Throughout the nearly one-and-a-half centuries of fishing activity on the island, the waters of Isle Royale have yielded millions of pounds of lake trout, whitefish, ciscoes, and lake herring to the nation's dinner tables.

At present there are only four commercial fishermen left on Isle Royale. They and several other private summer residents hold lifetime leases to their land, but when they are gone, there will be no more homes on the island. The lifetime lease arrangement was instituted when Isle Royale became a national park in 1940.

As a national park, Isle Royale is open from about May 15 through early October. During the summer season, boat transportation is available at Houghton and Copper Harbor in Michigan, and at Grand Portage, Minnesota.

Travelers from the Minnesota Arrowhead country can cross on either the daily trip of the *Wenonah* to Windigo or on the thrice weekly circumnavigation of the island by the *Voyager 2*.

Arrangements can be made with the captain of the *Voyager 2* to drop hikers at various campsites around the island, and to be met again at a later date. Or the hiker may take the *Voyager 2* to Rock Harbor at the northeast end of Isle Royale, hike the Greenstone Ridge Trail to Windigo, and take either boat back to Minnesota.

Turner Bus Company has daily service to Grand Portage on its Duluth to Thunder Bay run.

For more information on boat service to Isle Royale contact:
Grand Portage and Isle Royale transportation Company.
366 Lake Ave. South
Duluth, MN 55802
(218) 722-0945

National Park Service
Post Office Box 27
Houghton, MI 49931

Isle Royale Queen II
Copper Harbor, MI 49918
(906) 289-4337

For air service to Isle Royale contact:
Isle Royale Seaplane Service
Post Office Box 371
Houghton, MI 49931

Isle Royale National Park Trails

Daisy Farm Trail

This is a two mile long trail from the Greenstone Ridge Trail, running about four miles northeast of Chickenbone Lake to the Daisy Farm Lakeside Camp on Rock Harbor. The grade of this trail is less abrupt than any other trail that drops off the Greenstone Ridge, which is something you will appreciate when you walk back up this trail.

About a half a mile off the ridge the trail crosses a low, wet area, the headwaters of a stream flowing into Angleworm Lake. There is a slight rise in elevation, and then the path drops down into another swamp. The foot bridges across these wet areas allow the hiker to see the unique life of the swamps without getting soggy feet.

A mile from the Greenstone Ridge, the trail crosses Benson Creek, which comes out of Benson Lake. This creek is said to be a good place to fish for brook trout. The trail follows Benson Creek to the Daisy Farm Lakeside Camp. From 1847 to 1849, this was the site of an Ohio and Isle Royale mining camp. After the mining venture collapsed, the site was used as a sawmill, and then a garden for the Rock Harbor Lodge. As a garden, it grew daisies better than vegetables, hence the name Daisy Farm. During the Depression there was a Civilian Conservation Corps, or (CCC) camp here.

Feldtmann Ridge Trail

This is a fifteen mile-long trail into the swamps and ridges of the remote southwest corner of Isle Royale. This trail can be tied in with the five mile long Lake Trail and six miles of the Greenstone Ridge Trail to make a 26 mile-long loop trail out of Washington Harbor.

The trail starts at the Windigo Ranger Station, going along the shore of Washington Harbor until it turns inland at a small boat marker facing the harbor. A mile-and-a-half from the ranger station, Grace Creek is crossed on a bridge. One of the good things about Isle Royale is that all the streams and other wet places are crossed by bridges or planking, except on the Minong Ridge Trail. The swampy edges of Grace Creek are favored by cow moose with their calves. (There always seem to be a few around here.) A large beaver lodge is located downstream from the bridge.

After Grace Creek, a swamp is crossed on the first of a series of boardwalks. Without this planking it would be impossible to hike to Feldtmann Lake. The difficult wet, conditions of this section of trail is caused by the flat terrain that retains drainage.

The trail then crosses over the end of a low ridge covered by mature sugar maple and yellow birch. Past this, the trail returns to more swamp and boardwalk. One section of alder swamp at the east end of Feldtmann Lake is covered by a continuous 1,200 feet of planking, the longest boardwalk in the park.

As the trail turns towards Feldtmann Lake it parallels the red-colored conglomerate cliffs of the Feldtmann Ridge. This rock dates from the same geologic period as the deposit at Reservation River on the Minnesota shore. At the lower western end of the ridge near the shore of Feldtmann Lake, five miles from Windigo Station, there is a trail junction. A trail to the southwest goes a mile to meet the Feldtmann Portage Trail from Lake Superior. The trail to the east takes a turn up Feldtmann Ridge.

A mile down this ridge trail there is a low area to the south with a small beaver pond in it. However, most of this ridge, like other Isle Royale Ridges, is rather dry. It is covered by a scattered growth of birch, aspen, and mountain ash that furnishes good browse for Isle Royale's large moose herd. If it were not for the forest fires such as the 1936 fire that burned over a quarter of the island, there would not be such large amounts of browse and, consequently, the population of moose would not be as high.

At the Feldtmann Ridge fire tower, nine miles from Windigo Station, you can view many of the prominent points of interest: the Greenstone Ridge, Siskiwit Bay (named after a species of lake trout), and Lake Halloran.

From the tower it is another five miles to the Siskiwit Lakeside Camp. A mile or so beyond the tower the trail turns north and descends for nearly two miles before turning to the northeast. The lowland here was under water when the Siskiwit Ridge was separated from the main part of Isle Royale by a shallow channel. This part of the trail was an old logging road that was used for a few years before Isle Royale became a national park in 1940. A mile-and-a-half down this old logging road, a side trail takes off to the south, going to Lake Halloran. The chief feature of this almost rectangular lake is the wild lady's-slipper orchids that are found around its edges.

Just before reaching Siskiwit Bay, the trail goes through a large clearing that was the site of one of Isle Royale's CCC camps. The Siskiwit Bay Lakeside Camp has the usual shelters, grills, tables, and a large dock for those campers who arrive by boat.

Greenstone Ridge Trail

This is a 40 mile trail over the basalt backbone of Isle Royale, from Rock Harbor to Windigo Inn, almost the entire length of Isle Royale. This is not an easy trail to backpack and should only be attempted by those who have had some backpacking experience.

While the Greenstone Trail can be hiked from either end, it seems easier to backpack it from Rock Harbor, because of the steep grades at the Windigo Inn end of the trail. Starting at Rock Harbor, the trail follows the south shore of Tobin Harbor to the southeast end of the harbor, a distance of three miles. At the end of Tobin Harbor it turns to the west and crosses a stream. From here it is a gradual climb uphill towards Mount Franklin on the Greenstone Ridge. While most of the two-and-a-half-mile climb is a fairly easy grade, the last half mile is quite steep.

Mount Franklin, about 470 feet above Lake Superior, is named after Benjamin Franklin, whose efforts in negotiating the peace treaty with the British following the American Revolution resulted in Isle Royale becoming part of the United States. Once on Mount Franklin you have a good view of the northeastern end of Isle Royale, the outlying islands, and the Canadian Headlands. Although the ridge trails involve some steep hiking, the views make it worthwhile.

It is fairly level two-and-a-half miles of walking from Mount Franklin to the Mt. Ojibway fire tower. Naturally, all these fire towers have excellent views of the surrounding landscape. The trail to Daisy Farm slopes downward from this area. About a mile-and-a-quarter later, another trail leaves the ridge for Daisy Farm. Four trails converge on Daisy Farm Camp, the largest campground on Isle Royale. Here you will find shelters, grills, tables, and toilets.

A couple of miles farther on, the Greenstone Trail makes a sharp turn toward the north, going downhill over a creek. It then takes another sharp turn, this time southwesterly, and crosses a stream between Chickenbone and Livermore Lakes. Partway up a hill a side trail takes off to the northwest, going to Chickenbone Lake and its campground. Chickenbone Lake is another northern pike lake. You will find that the toughest going on this trail is walking back to the ridge from these lakeshore campgrounds.

From Chickenbone, the trail goes up and over a low hill, and across a level area for about a mile. It then crosses a small stream and climbs up Mount Siskiwit. This is not an easy walk. Just keep telling yourself that going straight up the steepest slope in sight is not a bad exchange for another fine viewpoint.

The rest of the seven mile walk to Hatchet Lake is easier hiking. At Hatchet Lake there is a standard Isle Royale Campground. This lake does not have northern pike, but there are some brook trout in it. If you have the proper tackle and/or skill and/or luck, you might hook and land a trout dinner.

After Hatchet Lake, it is four miles to the Ishpeming fire tower uphill, naturally! The fire tower is on the second highest peak on the island, 1,377 feet above sea level. From the fire tower it is two miles of downhill hiking to the cutoff to Desor Lake and its campground. Desor Lake is great wildlife territory. For some reason there seems to be more moose around Desor than any other lake on the Greenstone Trail. This lake is supposed to have brook trout, cisco, and whitefish.

From Desor Lake, the trail leads downhill for a short distance, over a fairly level area, and then back uphill to the highest point on Isle Royale. Mount Desor is 790 feet above the surface of Lake Superior. From the highest point on Mount Desor, it is a little over two-and-a-half miles to the junction with the Island Mine Trail.

The forest from here to Washington Harbor, six miles away, is an old climax sugar maple-yellow birch forest. Sugar Mountain, elevation 1,297, gets it name from the maple sap gathering and sugar making activities the Indians carried on here until 1847. Maple sugar was an important part of the Indians' diet.

The remainder of the trail is moderate, uphill-and-downhill hiking with a few wet spots here and there, until you arrive at the trail's end at Washington Harbor.

Greenstone Ridge Trail to Chippewa Harbor

This eight mile-long trail leaves the Greenstone Ridge Trail opposite the Chickenbone Campground eight miles from Rock Harbor. Because it touches the shores of three northern pike lakes, this is a good trail for fishermen to take.

The first lake is Lake Livermore, a short distance off the ridge. The trail crosses a small stream entering the lake at its eastern end. After passing this lake the trail continues toward Lake LeSage, up a ridge and down into a swamp to the south end of the lake.

From here there is a mile or so of trail to the north shore of Lake Richie. The trail follows the north shore of this wilderness lake in an easterly direction to a trail junction. The trail to the northeast goes two-and-a-half miles to Moskey Basin. The trail to the south continues around Lake Richie away from the shoreline to the southeast arm of the lake. From there it follows a stream to Chippewa Harbor Campground. A side trail goes a mile northeast to Lake Mason.

Hatchet Lake to Todd Harbor Trail

This four mile-long trail starts on the Greenstone Ridge Trail above Hatchet Lake. It drops off the ridge, goes by the Hatchet Lake Campground northeastward past Hatchet Lake for half-a-mile, and then, turning north, crosses a small stream. A short distance past this, a branch trail heads southwest to the north shore of Hatchet Lake, a good place to cast for trout.

The main trail continues north for a mile and joins the Minong Ridge Trail going east. After crossing another stream, it is a mile-and-a-half to the Todd Harbor Lakeside camp. Just before arriving at the camp, you pass by the Haytown Mine which was operated by the Pittsburgh and Isle Royale Mining Company from 1847 to 1853.

Huginnin Cove Loop Trail

This is an eight mile loop trail from the Washington Creek Trail to Huginnin Cove and back. It joins the Washington Creek Trail at two points. The first is a half mile northeast of the Washington Creek Campground, and the second is a half mile further on.

Starting at the latter point and going counterclockwise, the trail turns left going north over a small footbridge. After crossing a valley, the path heads northwest up a fairly steep hill and levels off.

When the trail nears the shore of Lake Superior, it turns southwest following a ridge. After about a mile along this ridge, the trail is crossed by a short north-south trail. The north trail goes a half mile to an overlook of the Lake Superior shoreline, and the south trail goes about the same distance to the headwaters of a small stream that flows into Huginnin Cove. This is another good place to see beavers at work. The trail follows the ridge into Huginnin Cove.

At Huginnin Cove Lakeside Camp, the path turns south and follows a wide glacial valley, crossing the small stream twice. After going back and forth across the valley, the trail heads southeast up and over a hill, and turns northeast along the banks of Washington Creek to a footbridge. After crossing the bridge, it is a short distance back to the Washington Creek Trail.

Ispeming Trail

This is a six-and-a-half-mile trail that starts from the Ispeming fire tower to the Malone Bay Lakeside Camp. The trail drops off the ridge at the fire tower, 14 miles northeast of Washington Harbor.

A mile from the tower, the trail crosses a bridge over a small stream. After going over a low hill and through a swampy area, the trail descends through a mature forest of oak, maple, and pine, that is a contrast to the usual mixed growth of early successional forests usually found on Isle Royale. These young forests are the result of the many forest fires that have swept over the island within historical times. Many of these fires were started by miners who were looking for surface indications of copper ore. A mile later the grade becomes less steep, and the trail leaves the climax forest, returning to recent burn areas of aspens, birch, and hazel brush.

The trail bottoms out near Siskiwit Lake and crosses two small streams in a swampy valley. The direction of the trail then turns to the northwest end and follows the shore of Siskiwit Lake for three-and-a-half-miles to the Siskiwit River. From here it follows the river to its outlet on Malone Bay, going by a beautiful cascade called Siskiwit Falls. The Malone Bay Lakeside Camp is a short walk rom the river outlet.

Island Mine Trail

This is a five mile-long trail from Siskiwit Lakeside Camp to the Greenstone Ridge Trail. From the campground, the first two miles of the trail follows the shore of Siskiwit Bay. The red-colored sand of this beach comes from the breakdown of the local sandstone that is found in the valleys of the island. The sandstone is very soft compared to the conglomerate of Feldtmann Ridge.

On the way around the bay the trail crosses two forks of the Big Siskiwit River, which drains Big Siskiwit Swamp. Later the trail goes across the neck of Senter Point, named after John J. Senter, a partner in the Siskiwit Mine operation. Past the point there is a half-mile of shore walking and the trail turns northwest, going inland.

Here, between the years 1873 and 1877 the Island Mine Company had a large mining camp and dock to service its mine up the ridge, two miles away. The first two miles of the trail to Greenstone Ridge Trail is built on the old wagon road from the camp to the mine. These old wagon roads usually make good hiking trails. The first mile on the wagon road goes through a wet lowland forest of spruce, fir, aspen, and alder. The trail then crosses Caribou Creek and goes uphill into a northern hardwood forest of maple and oak. After a mile of this you reach the Island Mine site. It is interesting to look around the old mining sites. But remember, these places can be dangerous, and it is against federal law to remove anything.

The wagon road ends at the mine; from here on the Greenstone Ridge Trail is a narrow footpath. For the next half-mile, there is a steep climb, then the trail drops down into the valley of the Little Siskiwit River, crossing two forks of this stream. From the valley, it is a short distance to the Greenstone Ridge Trail, six miles northwest of Washington Harbor.

McCargoe Cove Trail

This trail leaves the Greenstone Trail at the east end of Chickenbone Lake, and goes to the McCargoe Cove Lakeside Camp, a distance of two-and-a-quarter miles.

Between the years 1875 to 1879 this campground was the site of a large mining camp of the Minong Mining Company. The camp had homes, stores, a school house, teacher, and a resident physician. The mine that the camp served is about a mile west of the campground. At the old mine site, you can see pits, shafts, and other mining ruins, railway relics and large piles of rock.

Along the trail to the mine you can also see pits that were dug by prehistoric copper miners. Some of these pits have been dated as far back as 2,000 B.C. There are more of these ancient pits found around the McCargoe Cove area than any other part of Isle Royale.

From here the hiker may return to the Greenstone Ridge Trail by a trail around the west arm of Chickenbone Lake. Another route totry is the Minong Ridge Trail, which is a 26 mile walk to Washington Harbor.

Minong Ridge Trail

This 26 mile-long trail from Washington Harbor to McCargoe Cove was constructed as a manway in 1966. (A manway is a trail cut just wide enough for one man to pass on foot, providing access to the back country.) Later it was redesigned as the Minong Ridge Trail and opened to recreationists. However, it is still an unimproved trail without the bridges, boardwalks, and other construction found other Isle Royale hiking trails.

Because of the nature of this trail, it should only be attempted by experienced backpackers who are in condition to take on difficult terrain, biting insects, and uncertain weather without going crackers.

Starting the trail from the Washington end, take the Washington Creek Trail to the Windigo Mine Exploration site. The Minong Ridge Trail starts there. A short distance north of the mine site the trail crosses Washington Creek. As with all streams and swamps on this trail, those who can walk on water will have no problem. Those who can't, will get their feet wet.

After this crossing, the trail follows up the valley of a Washington Creek tributary. If you are interested in beaver, this is a favorable place to study them as well as the other wildlife that are attracted to beaver ponds.

After a mile or so in this beaver valley, the trail leaves, turning to the northeast. A mile further on, another tributary of Washington Creek is crossed. Don't bother changing socks after wading this stream, for you will have plenty of chances to get wet in the next six miles to the Lake Desor side trail.

Leaving Lake Desor, the next six miles to Little Todd Harbor side trail generally runs below the ridgeline. You can have some fine views by walking off the trail to the top of the ridge. This section of the trail has a little more elevation, so it may not be so wet. But, don't count on it, especially after an Isle Royale cloud burst.

For you beaver lovers, this part of the Minong Ridge Trail passes by two beaver ponds, where you should be able to see some of your furry little friends. Just hope their dams have not flooded the trail. These ponds are good places to look for moose and other wildlife.

A short distance past the second pond is the side trail to Little Todd Harbor. From here, the trail turns southeast, crosses two streams and returns to its northeast course, climbing up a ridge. After a mile on the ridge, the trail descends back to the lowlands and stays low until the side trail to Picket Bay is reached. There is a slight rise in elevation here. A mile further on, the Greenstone Ridge-Harbor trail joins in from the south. From this junction the trail crosses a stream and passes by a pond. Before reaching the Todd Harbor Lakeside Camp, the trail goes by the site of the Haytown Mine. After leaving the camp, the trail crosses a stream that flows out of Lake Harvey.

The last six miles of the trail from Todd Lake to McCargoe Cove stays mainly on the ridge going by Otter Lake and up to Pine Lake. From this point the trail descends to the McCargoe Cove Lakeside Camp.

From the campground, a trail to the southwest divides, with one trail proceeding to the west end of Chickenbone Lake, past its campground and on to the Greenstone Ridge Trail. The other trail bends around the northeast arm of Chickenbone Lake to the Greenstone Ridge Trail.

Mount Franklin to Lookout Louise

This is a five mile-long trail from Mt. Franklin to the northeastern end of the Greenstone Ridge Trail, although most Greenstone hikers usually get on or off at Mt. Franklin. From Mt. Franklin the trail follows the top of the ridge, giving the hiker some excellent views of this part of the island. Those who have hiked many miles through dense lowland forests without being able to see more than just a few yards in any direction will appreciate the scenery from the ridges of Isle Royale.

From Lookout Louise, the trail descends the ridge to Tobin Harbor, a mile away. On the way down, you pass Monument Rock, a 70-foot-high point of rock carved by waves of Glacial Lake Duluth.

Created by melting glaciers, Glacial Lake Duluth was the much larger and deeper predecessor to Lake Superior.

On the way down the hill keep your eyes peeled, the swamp around the beaver pond attracts a wide variety of Isle Royale wildlife. The trail ends on the shores of Tobin Harbor. There is no campground at the end of this trail.

Loop Trails

For those who wish to backpack a loop trail:

1. Minong Ridge Trail from Washington Harbor to McCargoe Cove, around Chickenbone Lake and back to Washington Harbor on the Greenstone Trail, a 55 mile-long loop.

2. The same trail, only turn onto the Greenstone Ridge Trail at Hatchet Lake, a loop of about 40 miles.

3. The Feldtmann Ridge Trail from Washington Harbor to Siskiwit Bay. The Island Mine Trail from there to Greenstone Ridge Trail, back to Washington Harbor, a 26 mile long loop.

4. Rock Harbor Lodge to Mt. Franklin, down the Greenstone Ridge Trail to Lake Livermore, to Lake Richie, to Moskey Basin, and back to Rock Harbor Lodge, a 30 mile-loop.

5. The same trail as above, only cut off the Greenstone Ridge Trail at Mt. Ojibway, go to Daisy Farm and back to Rock Harbor Lodge, this is a loop of 16 miles.

6. The Huginnin Cove Loop Trail, 8 miles.

VOYAGEURS NATIONAL PARK

This 220,000-acre land and water national park lies along the Minnesota-Ontario border east and north of U.S. Highway 53. The main access roads are Minnesota Highway 11, the Ash River Trail, and Saint Louis County Road 24. On the official state highway map the grid location is K-4.

Unlike many national parks, Voyageurs National Park does not have a well-developed road system providing access to the major visitor attractions. There are park roads to public facilities such as boat landings, public parking lots, and to the information center.

Except for the back country wilderness-type campsites, Voyageurs National Park does not have campgrounds. However, there are a number of state and privately operated campgrounds near the park's boundaries.

Lacking roads, travel in the park is by watercraft or on foot. Unlike the Boundary Waters Canoe Area of the neighboring Superior National Forest, there are few restrictions on the use of power craft on the park's four large lakes: 220,260-acre Rainy, 25,760-acre Kabetogama, 28,260-acre Namakan, and 8,890-acre Sand Point. However, the inland lakes of the Kabetogama Peninsula are restricted to human muscle-powered watercraft.

Voyageurs National Park does not have an extensive hiking trail system. Hiking is limited by a topography of streams, lakes, wetlands, and rocky ridges. Most of the park's 'land areas' are too wet for hiking trails. However, many of these wet areas have excellent cross-country ski trails.

Cruiser Lake Trail System

The Cruiser Lake Trail System, however, does offer some good hiking. It is made up of three loops, and linear trails crossing the east end of the Kabetogama Peninsula to connect Lake Kabetogama's Lost Bay with Rainy Lake's Andersons Bay.

The trailhead at the Lost Bay end of the trail is at the National Park Service dock at the east end of the bay. A quarter of a mile from the dock there is a junction of three trails. From this point a turn to the right (northeast) puts you on a trail up to an overlook above Lake Agnes. Cairns mark a spur trail down to the 40-acre lake's shoreline campsite. Continuing north on the main trail there is a junction with a trail that comes from the left (west). This trail is called the Agnes Lake Cutoff. It joins a trail loop of about two miles in length between Agnes and the 98-acre Ek Lake.

The main trail is to the north and runs to another junction with a trail from the west. This is the Overlook Trail, and as its name implies, it provides several scenic overlooks. The Overlook Trail, after turning south, joins the Lost Bay Trail by way of the east side of the South Ek Lake loop.

The Cruiser Lake Trail continues north across a stream and up a ridge to great views. There are more ridges until the trail snakes between two beaver ponds. An outstanding feature here is a 10 foot waterfall pouring water into a deep pool. Past the beaver ponds, it is up on a ridgeline onto the north side of Cruiser Lake. A spur trail to the left (southwest) leads to a campsite on Cruiser Lake. The campsite on this 120-acre lake is on an island connected to the mainland by a boardwalk.

The trail takes a north and then a northeastern bearing. A spur trail on the left (northwest) leads to a campsite on the southeast corner of 22-acre Brown Lake. This spur trail to Brown Lake descends from the ridgetop to the campsite in a series of switchbacks.

The Cruiser Lake Trail continues ridge crossings while turning northeast. After 130-acre Peary Lake comes into view there is a steep spur trail down to a lake campsite on a prominent point. The main trail is on the ridgeline above the east shoreline of Peary Lake.

Descending from the ridge, the trail enters a lowland forest and passes two beaver dam ponds. From here it is a short walk into the two mile-long Anderson Bay Loop. A short spur trail to the east leads to the shoreline of Rainy Lakes Anderson Bay.

Because the Anderson Bay Loop is on some high ridges above the waters and islands of Rainy Lake, it is probably one of the most scenic places in the park.

Ek Lake to Jorgens Lake Trail

From the Park Service dock on Lost Bay take the left branch of the trail junction heading left (west). The trail runs parallel to the Lost Bay shoreline, passing the water's edge at places with views of the bay. Soon after, the trail comes to a junction. The left trail (northwest) goes to the south shore of Ek Lake. There the Ek Lake-to-Lost Bay portage trail is crossed. Beyond the portage is a board-walk crossing of wetland, then it is up to a ridge with a full view of Ek lake. After going down and by the lake's shoreline, the trail ascends a bluff above the lake and then returns to the shoreline. About halfway along the lakeshore, a spur trail to the right (north) ends at a lakeshore campsite.

The main trail runs downward and crosses a stream on park planking. After the crossing, the trail joins in and becomes part of the Lost Bay-to-Quarter Line Lake and Jorgens Lakes portage. A spur trail to the right (east) ends at a campsite on the west end of Quarter Line Lake.

The trail continues to 64-acre Jorgens Lake, crossing three ridges with wetlands in between bridged by boardwalks, before ending at a lakeside campsite.

The big drawback of the Cruiser Lake Trail System is that you have to travel across Rainy or Kabetogama Lakes to hike the trails. Leaving a boat or canoe unattended while hiking may not be a good idea. However, it is possible to contact park concessionaires who operate tour boats on the four main lakes. They can make arrangements with you for a drop-off and pick-up time.

For Rainy Lake contact:

Rainy Lake Cruises
Route 8, P.O. Box 303
International Falls, MN 56649
(218) 286-5470

For Kabetogama Lake contact:
Voyageur National Park Pleasure Cruises
1116 1st Ave, East
International Falls, MN 56649
(218) 283-8264

For further information contact:
Superintendent
Voyageurs National Park
P.O. Box 50
International Falls, MN 56649
(218) 283-9821

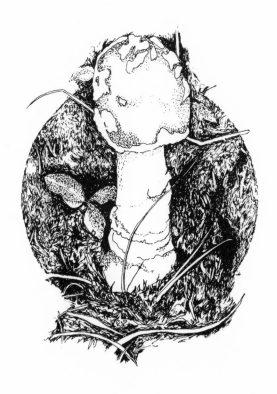

Arrowhead State Forest Trails

Fon Du Lac State Forest

Fond Du Lac State Forest Ski Trail System

This cross country ski trail system is fairly good for off-season hiking. The trails are well marked and there are many "you are here" signs at trail intersections. There are no large areas of wet trail as there are on many ski trails.

To reach these trails, take State Highway 210 from Duluth to Cromwell. At Cromwell drive north on County Road 120. Follow this road for about four and a half miles, passing by the snowmobile trail trailhead and the nearby DNR Forestry fire tower, and continuing for another mile to the turn into the ski trail parking lot. On the official state highway map its grid location is L-10.

The trails

The Fond Du Lac ski trail system is made up of seven loops, with a total of 11 miles of trail. As is true of many ski trail systems, the trails are graded from easy to most difficult.

Part of the system is made up of recently constructed recreation trails, while other parts follow the routes of the roads developed by the settlers who attempted to farm the area in the 1920's. Like many efforts to farm cut-over forest, it ended in failure. Most of these farms were returned to state ownership due to nonpayment of taxes.

The Fond Du Lac State Forest is one of many state forests that were created from tax-forfeited land.

Because there are no campsites in this trail system, it should be regarded as a day-use only area.

For a map and other information contact:
Area Forest Supervisor
Box 220 Highway 33 South
Cloquet, MN 55720
(218) 879-4544

Nemadji State Forest

National Christmas Tree Trail

This trail, located in the Nemadji State Forest south of Duluth, is a excellent example of what can be done in recreational trail development in our Minnesota State Forests.

The Nemadji State Forest is a working forest that produces forest products as well as recreational opportunities. The National Christmas Tree Trail, besides being on interesting trail for its examples of wildlife and forest management practices, is also a relaxing trail to walk.

The trail starts from Gafvert Campground on Pickerel Lake. To reach this campground turn east off of Minnesota Highway 23 onto County Road 146. Drive south on this road for about a quarter of a mile, and then turn east on County Road for a mile. Next turn south on the Net Lake Road for a mile and a quarter. This will take you around the west shore of Net Lake and by the road that leads into the campground. On the offical state highway map its grid location is L-11.

The campground has nine campsites with fire rings, tables, water pumps, and pit toilets. Adjacent to the camping area are the day-use facilities. These include picnic sites, watercraft access to the 57-acre Pickerel Lake, and the trailheads for both the snowmobile and foot trails.

The Nemadji State Forest now produces a crop of forest products. This was not always so. In the early years of this century, logging removed much of the forest cover. Afterwards, settlers moved in to try farming the cut-over land. Due to soil and market conditions these efforts failed. Most of the land was returned to state ownership due to nonpayment of taxes. Later the Nemadji State Forest was established.

At the present time there are a few scattered groves of white pine. But most of the forest is second growth. The higher, drier areas of Nemadji State Forest grow mainly aspen, birch, maple, oak, spruce, and fir. The lower and wetter soils support trees such as black spruce, tamarack, white cedar, and ash. The variety of plant cover provides many species of wildlife with a range of habitats.

The Trail

The National Christmas Tree Trail is named after a huge white spruce that was harvested from the forest and placed in front of the White House in 1977.

The trailhead is marked by a sign at a point just north of the camping area. The trail system is made up of the main loop plus two short spur trails, one leading to an old beaver dam site on the banks of the Net River, and the other to the boggy shoreline of 58 acre Cranberry Lake.

Because the trail passes through a working forest it is possible to see modern forest management at work. The large, open area on the first part of the trail is the result of clear-cutting a stand of mature aspen and birch. With the old trees removed, the site was planted with red pine and white spruce seedlings. It is the start of a new forest. Another interesting area is a twenty-year-old stand of aspen that regenerated from sprouting after the old trees were removed in a clear-cut logging operation. Towards the end of the loop there is the place where the 1977 National Christmas Tree was removed. Five white spruce trees have been planted where the Christmas Tree stood.

Because the trail is very level it would be an excellent cross country ski trail for beginning skiers.

For a map and further information contact:
Area Forest Supervisor
Route 2,701 South Kenwood
Moose Lake, MN 55767
(218) 485-4474

ARROWHEAD STATE PARK
TRAILS

The Minnesota State Park system has some of the best hiking trails in Minnesota. All state parks in the Arrowhead Region have favorable wildlife habitats that support high populations of common Minnesota birds and mammals. To get up-to-date information on any state park trail call 1-800-652-9747, and ask for the (DNR) Department of Natural Resources, State Park Division; or call the individual state park office.

BANNING STATE PARK

This great riverside park is four miles northeast of the city of Sandstone. From I-35 turn east on Minnesota Highway 23 for three miles. The grid location on the official state highway map is L-12.

The park has a 31-site rustic campground, 4 canoe campsites, three small boat landings and a seven site picnic area with 15 tables.

The Kettle River is 80 miles long and flows through a wide range of terrain, including 10 miles of Banning State Park, before entering into the Saint Croix River at Saint Croix State Park.

The Kettle River is a translation from the Ojibway name *Akiko sibi* for the round kettle-shaped depressions that can be seen in the rock outcroppings in the riverbed. These strange looking holes are formed when the river current spins stones in a fracture in the soft sedementary rock of the riverbed.

In 1975 the Kettle River was designated a Minnesota Wild and Scenic River in recognition of its value as a recreational resource. The river is also a state canoe route and is known as a whitewater challenge for kayakers.

In the past, the area forest was dominated by large stands of white pine, but intensive logging and the fire of 1894 reduced most of the great trees to stumps and ashes. In time the land was reforested by nature with a second growth of northern hardwood species such as basswood, maple, elm, aspen, birch, and oak.

Banning State Park is named after the 1896 town site of Banning, which was named after William L. Banning. Mr. Banning was born in Wilmington, Delaware in 1814. In 1855 he moved to St. Paul, served in the Third Minnesota Regiment in the Civil War, and later was a Saint Paul businessman and railroad contractor. He was also president of the Saint Paul and Duluth Railroad. He died in St. Paul in 1893.

Banning was a hamlet on a branch of the Northern Pacific Railroad. In 1900 the population of Banning was about 300. Its main economic activity was a rock quarry that at one time employed more than 500 stonecutters. The quarry provided Kettle River Sandstone for the construction of many Twin City buildings, including the Minneapolis City Hall. Kettle River Sandstone gave the nearby town of Sandstone its name. In 1903 an asphalt plant was built next to the quarry.

Prosperity for the town of Banning came to an end with the development of structural steel, which replaced the use of large stone blocks. Shortly after the closing of the quarry, the asphalt plant shut down. In a few years the site of the town of Banning was farmland. Now all that can be seen by the visitor are the walls and foundations of the town power plant.

Trails

Banning State Park has about 14 miles of hiking trails. The trails cover a wide range of terrain, ranging from riverside trails to loop trails through the aspen-birch brush, which is excellent wildlife habitat. Except for the riverside trail to Wolf Creek Falls that ends at Robinson Park in the town of Sandstone, all of the Banning State Park trails are loop trails.

One trailhead for the system is at the information center, located at the park entrance. From here trails lead east, where there are two loop trails. One circles through the woods, while the other's east side follows along the Kettle River to a boat ramp site.

Another trailhead is at the park campground. From this trailhead, hikers can walk north to the information center or go on another trail in the same direction to the picnic area. Trails to the east lead to trails above and alongside the famous Banning Rapids, with great views of a famous whitewater stretch of the river.

Banning State Park has done a first class job in developing its trail system. There are enough trails here for a full weekend of good hiking.

For a map and other information contact:
Park Manager
Banning State Park
P.O. Box 'V'
Sandstone, MN 55072
(612) 245-2668

BEAR HEAD LAKE STATE PARK

Bear Head Lake State Park is located 16 miles west of Ely on Highway 169. The state highway map grid location is M-7. This 4,100-acre park is near the edge of the Boundary Waters Canoe Area. The park's main body of water, the 693-acre Bear Head Lake, has the look of a "Canoe Country" lake, with many bays and islands. Most of the park's development is in the pennisula between the North and East Bays of Bear Head Lake. There are 24 semi-modern campsites, 49 rustic campsites, four backpacking campsites, and a pioneer group camp for organizations. Rental canoes and boats are available at the park.

The Trails

Bear Head Lake State Park has about 17 miles of trails that mainly form loops around Cub and Norberg lakes and the north shore of the East Bay of Bear Head Lake. The Taconite State Corridor Trail passes through the park. A new trail leads southward from the group campground to backpacker campsites on 60-acre Becky and 130-acre Blueberry lakes.

For a map and other information contact:
Park Manager
Bear Head Lake State Park
Star Route 2, Box 5700
Ely, MN 55731
(218) 365-4253

CASCADE RIVER STATE PARK

Cascade River State Park is located 10 miles southwest of Grand Marais on the Northshore Highway 61. On the state highway map its grid location is Q-7. The park is 2,800-acres of scenic hills and shoreline. Cascade River is named for the series of beautiful waterfalls near its mouth. The river drains a number of inland lakes, including Cascade, Little Cascade, Swamp, Eagle, Zoo, and Island lakes.

Taking advantage of the spectacular Cascade River scenery, the U.S. Forest Service developed the Cascade River Trail which was built in the 1930's by Civilian Conservation Corps (CCC). It is a fairly rugged trail that goes up the west side of the Cascade River and comes down the east side of the river, making a five mile loop. In the Cascade River's last three miles there is a drop of 900 feet, creating scores of waterfalls and rapids.

Other trails developed by the Cascade River State Park cover a wide range of terrain, from level lakeside trails that can be walked by any age group, to demanding trails that climb up to the ridgetops, with outstanding views of Lake Superior and the forested North Shore. Some of the high overlooks have Adirondack-type, three-sided shelters that may be used by backpackers as walk-in campsites.

In the winter most of these hiking trails are cross-country ski trails.

The state park here has a 30 unit modern campground, complete with flush toilets and showers. The famous Cascade Lodge, which is a short distance west of the river, offers a good place to stay, as well as a restaurant.

For a map and other information contact:
Park Manager
Cascade River State Park
East Star Route Box 45
Lutsen, MN 55612
(218) 387-1543

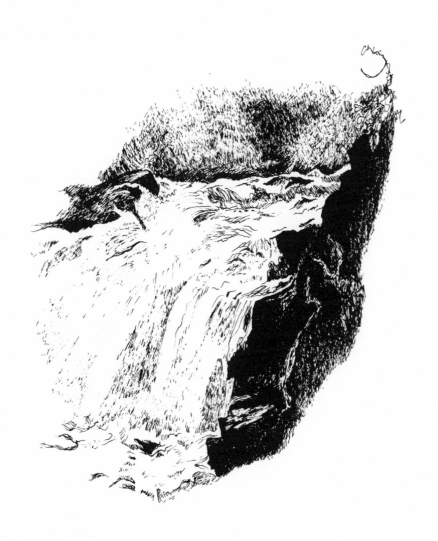

GEORGE H. CROSBY-MANITOU STATE PARK

George H. Crosby-Manitou State Park is located eight miles northeast of Finland on County Highway 7. On the state highwap map it grid location is O-8. Take the Route 1 turnoff of Finland from the North Shore Highway to Finland. This North Shore Park features backpacking campsites along the fast flowing Manitou River. The Indians knew this river as *Manidoobimadga-zibi* which means "spirit" or "ghost." This may be because of the appearance of heavy mists seen around the falls and rapids.

The park is listed as a backpacking park, however, it has received so much use from backpackers that it is in danger of overuse. Having only 15 backpacking campsites by the river, and five walk-in campsites on or near 21-acre Bensen Lake. There is also a small picnic area next to the lake. In this writer's opinion, the best way to walk this park is by day-hiking it, while staying overnight at one of the nearby public or private campgrounds or resorts. You could spend several days hiking the trails here. There are three loops, ranging in length from six to 15 miles along the Manitou River. All three loops begin and end at the park's parking lot. In addition, spur trails lead off from the loops to hills with scenic viewpoints of the mighty Manitou River as it tumbles to Lake Superior, carving the deepest canyon along the North Shore.

The trails are tough, rugged, and mountainous, and they will test your hiking boots. You will need to carry a day pack for hiking these trails, with extra clothing in case there is a cold wind off of the lake. Take plenty to drink, as the only safe water is at the park office. The water from the Manitou River and Bensen Lake must be treated or boiled.

For a map and other information contact:
Park Manager
George Crosby State Park
Box 482
Finland, MN 55603
(218) 226-3539

GOOSEBERRY FALLS STATE PARK

Gooseberry Falls State Park is 13 miles northeast of Two Harbors, on North Shore Highway 61. Its highway grid location is N-19. The name Gooseberry is said to a translation of the Ojibway *Shab-on-im-i-kan-Zibil* or "place of the Gooseberries river." The park's campground has 70 modern sites and three walk-in campsites. It is the most popular North Shore state park in terms of numbers of visitors. It has 18 miles of trails, including a 1.5 mile long self-guided nature trail that offers the visitor views of Gooseberry River gorges and waterfalls, as well as Lake Superior shoreline. The paths at this park are clearly marked with numbered intersections and "you are here" maps. The trails most favored by visitors are those that follow the Gooseberry River and offer grand views of the falls and rapids. In the winter season many of the trails are open to cross-country skiing and feature trail shelters.

Because there is so much to see at this park, the best way to do it would be to stay overnight at the Gooseberry State Park Campground and take a full day or more to hike the trails. Incidentally, Gooseberry ranks as one of the best hiking spots for families with small children.

For a map and other information contact:
Park Manager
Gooseberry Falls State Park
1300 Highway 61 East
Two Harbors, MN 55146
(218) 834-3855

INTERSTATE STATE PARK

This very popular little Saint Croix River Valley state park is at the junction of U.S. Highway 8 and Minnesota State Highway 95 in Taylors Falls. Its grid location on the official state highway map is L-15.

The beautiful Saint Croix River forms this part of the Minnesota-Wisconsin border. On each side of the river at Taylors Falls is a state park named Interstate. When established in 1895, the Wisconsin park was that state's first state park. The Minnesota Interstate was Minnesota's second state park.

The Minnesota Interstate is the far smaller of the two parks, with 293-acres, compared to the 1,734-acres of its larger neighbor. The two state parks carry on cooperative programs serving the public need for outdoor education and recreation.

There are two areas of development in the Minnesota Interstate Park, a northern unit and a southern unit.

The Northern Unit

The Northern Unit is in the town of Taylors Falls, where there is a contact station, an interpretive center, a refectory, and the ticket office for river excursions.

For many visitors, Interstate Park is most remembered for the Saint Croix River excursion boat trips. From the time they leave the docks at Taylor's Falls until they return, excursion boat passengers travel past outstanding views of the famous Delles of the Saint Croix.

Once an older river, the mighty Glacial River Saint Croix, poured melt waters of retreating glaciers through this valley. Glacial River Saint Croix carried a much larger volume of water than does the present river. It carved the high canyon walls into strange shapes that seem to resemble the beings and places of a mythical world.

Along the way, the excursion boat skipper points out some of the more significant features of the route. This river excursion tour is one of the best in the nation and should not be missed. The tour of the Dells alone is well worth a trip to Interstate Park.

Excursion boats are not the only recreational watercraft that ply the Interstate Parks section of the Saint Croix River. On any summer day the visitor will see a number of small craft. Some of these recreationists bring their own, while others rent. Many visitors like to putter around and try fishing in park waters, others voyage further away on the Saint Croix River. For those voyagers who would like to camp out along the river there are a number of campsites available, including some in state parks.

The Saint Croix River is designated a National Wild and Scenic River and is administrated by the National Park Service.

The Southern Unit

The Southern Unit is about a mile-and-a-half south of Taylors Falls, off the highway. This unit is the location of the park naturalist station, the picnic area, and the campground. The campground is on a large open field. Because the campground is only 30 miles from the Twin Cities it is one of the most heavily used in the state park system. Every summer weekend it is filled to capacity with camping shelters ranging from motor homes to nylon pup tents.

The Pothole Trail

Located in the Northern Unit, the nature trail of Minnesota's Interstate Park is named the Pothole Trail. It is a self-guided quarter of a mile loop around a group of potlike holes that were formed by the rapids of the Glacial River Saint Croix.

Pebbles and sand rotating in swirling eddies drilled potlike holes in the glacial river's bedrock. One of these potholes along the Pothole Trail is 60 feet deep.

Rental tape recorders that provide interpretation of this trail are available at the park refectory.

River Trail

This mile-and-a-half linear riverside trail connects the Northern and Southern units of the park. From the south end of the parking lot in Taylors Falls the River Trail heads uphill to follow along the highway. Along the way there are two scenic overlooks of the river valley. Past the second overlook the trail gradually slopes downward to parallel the river, passing through a deciduous forest before ending at the campground.

Curtain Falls Trail

This two-and-a-quarter-mile-long loop trail in the Southern Unit starts northwest of the campground contact station and passes under the highway through a short tunnel. Across the highway, the trail runs up the valley of Curtain Creek through a great hardwood forest. The steeper parts of the trail have stairways made of large flat rocks.

Partway up, the trail passes through two large concrete pillars that are capped by large rock slabs. These pillars were part of a railroad that used to run through the Saint Croix Valley. Excursion trains transported weekend recreationists from the Twin Cities to Taylors Falls.

The Curtain Falls Trail is a wide trail that seems to have been used by walkers for many years. On the way up the creek valley, the trail crosses tributary streams on strong stone bridges. The creek bed is filled with huge boulders and logs.

At the Curtain Falls site, the trail turns away from the creek and uphill past a large half-dome sandstone formation. Past this there is a steep rise a short distance to the ridgeline. From the ridge overlooks there are some outstanding views of the Saint Croix River Valley. The trail stays on top of the ridge until it returns via another creek valley to the highway across from the Southern Unit entrance.

For a map and other information contact:
Park Manager
Interstate State Park
Taylors Falls, MN 55084
(612) 465-5711

JAY COOKE STATE PARK

Jay Cooke State Park is located two miles west of Duluth on Highway 210. Its grid location on the state highway map is L-10.

Jay Cooke was born in August, 1821 in Sanddusky, Ohio and died in Ogontz, Pennsylvania in February, 1905. During the Civil War he was the principal financial agent for the federal government. In the Panic of 1873, he lost his fortune. But after a time in retirement he returned to business and made an even greater fortune. Mr. Cooke was a sportsman who spent much of his time in his later years hunting and fishing.

In 1915 the estate of Jay Cooke donated more than 2,000-acres on both sides of the St. Louis River to be preserved by the State of Minnesota as a park for the recreation of the people. This was the start of Jay Cooke State Park.

Topographically speaking, the 8,813-acre Jay Cooke State Park is like a deep bowl that is filled with a hardwood forest surrounded by a ring of ridges, with the St. Louis River flowing through it. The forest vegetation and abundant supply of fresh water create excellent habitat for the 46 species of mammals and 173 species of birds that can seen in the park. Besides the usual Minnesota forest denizens, there are frequent reports of mountain lion or cougar seen in or near the park.

Jay Cooke has a modern, 94-site campground located near park headquarters. There are two large picnic areas. One is next to the park office, and the other is several miles east, on Oldenberg Point, a scenic area overlooking the Saint Louis River valley.

One of the most popular visitor attractions of the park is the swinging bridge over the St. Louis River. The present bridge is the third built at this site. The first was built in 1930 by a Civilian Conservation Corps (CCC) work crew. It was washed out by floodwaters in 1950. The bridge was rebuilt in 1954. In 1972, flood waters again destroyed it, and then was reconstructed in 1979. Most of the time there is little flowing under the bridge, and a person looking down from it will see more dry rock than water. By the way, the river below the bridge is said to be good fishing waters.

The park has an interesting interpretive center, with a small museum from which a park naturalist conducts a summer program.

In the 1950's when I first visited Jay Cooke State Park, the park had very little to offer the public except a picnic area. There were no hiking trails. Now the park has over 40 miles of well-marked hiking trails in excellent walking condition which is true of most state park trails. There are numbered intersections with "you are here" maps on them to aid recreationists. The paved Munger State Trail passes through the northern part of the park and is connected to the park trails, and a recent addition is a 12 mile-long system of mountain bike trails.

For a map and further information contact:
Park Manager
Jay Cooke State Park
500 East Highway 210
Carlton, MN 56718
(218) 384-4610

Mountain and touring bike rental:
Superior Outdoors
(218) 384-4637

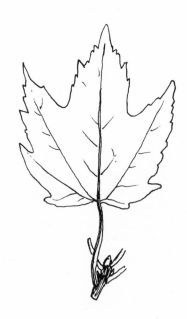

JUDGE C. R. MAGNEY STATE PARK

This 4,514-acre north shore state park is about 14 miles northeast of Grand Marais on Highway 61. Its highway map grid location is R-6. It was formerly known as the Brule River State Park. The Ojibway Indians named the river *Wissakode-zibi* or "Half-burnt-wood river."

This grand state park offers six miles of good trails for family hiking. The trails take you up the river to some unusual geological formations, such as the Devil's Kettle, as well as scenic vistas of the Brule River Gorges.

At the the Devil's Kettle, half the Brule River water flows into a kettle hole eroded in the rock. Presumably, the flow rejoins the main river, but no one knows exactly where. Dye poured into the hole appears in Lake Superior but not in the river.

There is a 38-unit campground at the park. An interesting place to stay while hiking the Judge C. R. Magney State Park is the Naniboujou Lodge, located across the highway from the park entrance and at the mouth of the Brule River. The lodge was built in the 1920's as a private club. Two well-known members were Jack Dempsey and Babe Ruth. The food served is extraordinary. The spring and fall fishing is, too.

For a map and further information contact:
Park Manager
Judge C.R. Magney State Park
Grand Marais, MN 55604
(218) 387-2929

McCARTHY BEACH STATE PARK

Located 20 miles north of Hibbing on St. Louis County Road 5, highway map grid K-7, this 2,566-acre park is mainly a day use facility. Its biggest attractions are the waters of Sturgeon, Side, and Beatrice lakes.

Most of the development of the park is in the narrow strip of land between Side and Sturgeon Lakes. Here you will find the information center, and the main 60 site campground, boat ramps, and picnic areas. A rustic campground and boat ramp is northwest of 2,050-acre Sturgeon Lake on the shores of Beatrice Lake.

Most outdoor recreation at McCarthy Beach State Park is day use activities such as swimming, boating, and fishing. Rental boats are available.

Trails

There are 18 miles of foot trails in the park, mainly in loops along glacial ridges and through narrow valleys. The trail intersections are numbered and have "you are here" maps to orient the hiker. The State Taconite Corridor Trail passes through the park.

For a map and further information contact:
Park Manager
McCarthy Beach State Park
HCR 5, Box 341
Hibbing, MN 55746
(218) 254-2411

MOOSE LAKE STATE PARK

This 965-acre recreation area is located on Carlton County Road 137 about a mile east of Interstate-35 and two miles east of the town of Moose Lake. The state highway map grid location is L-11. There is a parking lot, an 18-site campground, a picnic area, a swimming beach, and a boat landing, all on or near the northeast bay of Echo Lake. While popular as a day use area for picnicking and boating and as a good place to stay overnight while enroute to somewhere else, this recreation area is also regarded as an un-crowded weekend retreat.

Trails

There are about four miles of hiking trails in the recreation area that follow the shoreline of 112-acre Echo Lake and loop around the hills. In the winter these are cross-country ski trails.

For a map and further information contact:
Park Manager
Moose Lake
1000 County Road 137
Moose Lake, MN 55767
(218) 485-4059

ST. CROIX STATE PARK

St. Croix State Park is located 16 miles east of Hinckley on Highway 48. Its state highway map grid location is L-13. This St. Croix River park is the largest Minnesota state park, with more than 34,000-acres. It was developed during the 1930's by the Natonal Park Service as the St. Croix Recreation Demonstration Area.

Because it is the largest state park, and close to the state's population centers, St. Croix State Park is also Minnesota's most developed state park. For campers, the park has backpacking campsites, walk-in campsites, canoe campsites, a primitive group campground, a semi-modern campground, and modern group camp complexes. Who could ask for anything more?

Besides the vast park forest, the other natural attraction here is the St. Croix River. This beautiful river is both a Minnesota Canoe Route and a National Scenic Riverway. The river forms the park's 21-mile east border and provides recreation for canoeists, boaters, and fishermen.

Trails

The terrain of St. Croix State Park, with its extensive forest cover and waterways, provides an excellent place for trails. The topography here is quite level, making the bluffs overlooking the St. Croix and Kettle rivers the only scenic overviews in the park.

There are 127 miles of hiking and multi-use trails in the park. The trail system includes two miles of easy walking trail that can be used by those in wheelchairs or pushing a stroller. There is a six mile long bike path. In the winter there is 21 mile-long cross-country ski trail that loops through pine forests and along the St. Croix River. Seventy-five miles of horseback riding trail are used by snowmobilers in the winter. A 23 mile-long trail system along the St. Croix and Kettle Rivers has been developed for hikers.

The trails in St. Croix State Park vary from narrow paths to 10 foot-wide, multi-use trails.

The Minnesota-Wisconsin Boundary State Corridor Trail passes through the park.

For a map and further information contact:
Park Manager
St. Croix State Park
Route 3, Box 174
Hinckley, MN 55037   (612) 384-6591

SAINT CROIX WILD RIVER STATE PARK

This very scenic 6,706-acre state park is located in the beautiful Saint Croix River Valley about 50 miles from downtown Saint Paul. From I-35W, turn east onto State Highway 95 for 12 miles. Turn left (north) onto County Road 12 for another six miles to the park entrance. On the official state highway map the grid location is K-14.

Saint Croix Wild River State Park is one of five state parks situated along the banks of the beautiful Saint Croix River. This river is part of the National Wild and Scenic System under the administration of the National Park Service. Saint Croix Wild River State Park's name comes from the designation of the St. Croix as a wild and scenic river.

Today, the Saint Croix River is very popular with anglers and canoeists as well as power boaters. In the past it was a highway for the canoes of the Dakotah, Fox, Saux, and Ojibway, as well fur traders and explorers.

Because Saint Croix Wild River State Park is one of the more recently developed Minnesota state parks, its planners were able to incorporate some of the latest designs in visitor facilities. The park's two story interpretive center is set on a ridgetop overlooking the Saint Croix River. The story of the park, past and present, is presented in many interesting displays. From the center's wide river front facing deck, there is a magnificent view of the river and valley. An interesting feature of the interpretative center is the wildlife museum, which displays mounted specimens of park wildlife.

Ample campsites are available in the park's modern drive-in campground, as well as campgrounds for horseback riders and groups such as scouts. In addition to campgrounds there also are remote campsites for backpackers and canoeists.

Because it is so close to the Twin Cities and its location on the banks of the Saint Croix River, the park is an ideal location for picnics. To service this need, a modern picnic area has been developed, with a large shelter that has four fireplaces, electric lighting, and a wide deck that overlooks the Saint Croix River. There are also picnic sites dotted along the riverbank.

For those looking for water recreation, there is a boat landing.

St. Croix Wild River State Park offers a nature interpretive program that is conducted by naturalists. In addition to giving illustrated lectures, the naturalists guide visitors on walks through different areas of the park. These nature walks take place both during daylight hours and after dark.

Most of the park's forest is now second growth hardwood. The forests of huge white pine that once filled the Saint Croix River Valley were cut down long ago. There is never a loss without some gain, however. The gain in this case is that hardwood forests are generally better habitats for many species of wildlife. A walk in the Wild River State Park may be rewarded by a sighting of deer, grouse, rabbit, squirrel, or woodcock.

The Trails

St. Croix Wild River State Park has about 35 miles of hiking trails, which are also used for cross-country skiing. In addition, there are 20 miles of horse trails.

As with many Minnesota parks, the best place to start walking is on a nature trail, guided by a park naturalist. At Wild River State Park the one-mile nature trail is named Amik's Pond. *Amik* is an Ojibway name for the beaver. This trail is best reached from the interpretive center. Take the hiking trail downhill from the center for a short distance to where the trail to Amik's pond branches off to the left. This trail is a loop on the flood plain, and it is often inundated during periods of high water.

The trail passes through a deciduous forest made up of mainly willow, paper birch, and aspen. Aspen bark is the beavers' main food, and they cannot live where the tree does not grow.

Beaver ponds, such as Amik's are a good place to observe wildlife. In addition, to those species that live in the ponds, there are others that use the ponds as sources of food and water.

For many visitors, the most rewarding hike is the River Side Trail where there are beautiful views of the river valley. One of the points of interest along this trail is the site of the Nevers Dam. It is about a mile north of the boat landing. The Nevers Dam was built in 1889 by the Saint Croix Dam and Boom Company to aid in floating logs down the river. Constructed of wood, it was said to have been the largest pile-driven dam in the world.

To the day hiker and the backpacker, Wild River State Park offers a wide range of hiking experiences through a variety of terrain, ranging from flat grassland to steep, hilly forests.

For a map and further information contact:
St. Croix Wild River State Park
Rt 1, Box 75
Center City, MN 55012
(612) 583-2125

SAVANNA PORTAGE STATE PARK

Savanna Portage State Park is located 18 miles north of McGregor on County Road 65. It grid location is J-10. This 15,818-acre park is the third largest in the state park system, covering an area that includes lakes, swamps, and hills. A 60-unit campground is located on 80-acre Shumway Lake. There are also accommodations available at area resorts and motels.

Because of the low, wet nature of much of the park land, most of the 22 miles of the trail system circles around the hilly area between Shumway and 32-acre Loon lakes.

The historic Savanna Portage Trail is six miles long, beginning at the historical marker at the parking lot. The trail starts by going through a mixed coniferous and deciduous forest and passing over some small streams and around low hills in a northeasterly direction. This first part of the trail is very pleasant hiking.

The path then plunges into a black spruce and tamarack forest on its way to the headwaters of the East Savanna River, and it gets wetter and wetter before you reach the Voyageurs Canoe Landing. You will find yourself on park planking to keep your feet dry. After a while, you can see why the Voyageurs were paid extra to transport goods over this portage.

Because of the low, wet, buggy nature of this trail and the lack of a camping facility at the east end of the portage, it should be day hiking only. Camp at the Green Lake auto campground or the Remote Lake backpacking campground, a mile west of the picnic area on a good trail.

Because most of the land in this part of Minnesota is very low, wet, and productive of biting insects, it is the better part of valor to leave hiking the Savannah Portage State Park Trails until late summer or early fall, when hiking conditions can be much better.

For a map and further information contact:
Park Manager
Savanna Portage State Park
Rt. 3, Box 326
McGregor, MN 55760

SCENIC STATE PARK

Scenic State Park is located seven miles southwest of the town of Big Fork on Highway 7. Its map grid is I-7. This popular state park covers 2,922-acres of forest and lake. Because of the efforts of local residents, the park was developed in the 1920's to preserve some stands of huge red and white pine. It was one of Minnesota's first state parks.

The park has two main campgrounds, with 120 semi-modern and 30 rustic campsites. There is also a primitive group campground with canoe access on 62-acre Lake of the Isles. There are 12 backpacking campsites, and six walk-in campsites for canoeists on the shores of 595-acre Coon and Sandwick lakes. Rental canoes and boats are available at the park. A summer naturalist program offers visiters opportunities to learn about the natural world of the park.

Trails

Scenic State Park has about 14 miles of hiking trails, which wind around Coon and Sandwick lakes. These two lakes are connected by such a wide channel that seem seem to be one body of water. Other side trails lead to the primitive group camp of Lake of the Isles, and to Pine and Tell lakes where there are backpacking campsites.

The Chase Point Trail is the outstanding trail of the park. This peninsula between Coon and Sandwick Lakes is a long, narrow esker, formed during the ice age from sand and gravel that was deposited from a river that flowed through a glacier. When the glacier melted, the sand gravel was left. It is interesting to note the differances in the vegetation on this ridge. One side has an abundant growth of many species of plants, while the other side is comparatively barren.

For a map and further informaton contact:
Park Manger
Scenic State Park
Bigfork, MN 55616
(218) 743-3362

SPLIT ROCK LIGHTHOUSE STATE PARK

This 1,872-acre state park is on the North Shore of Lake Superior off the North Shore Highway 61. It is 20 miles north of the city of Two Harbors. Its grid location on the official state highway map is O-9.

The park commemorates its namesake, the famous lighthouse built near a split-rock faced cliff above Lake Superior, which was named after the parks main stream, the Split Rock River. The Indian name for the river was *Gin-in-wag-i-ko-zibi* from the appearance of large quantities of split rock on high bluffs east of the river. The lighthouse was built in 1910 and remained operational until 1969.

The Minnesota Historical Society now administers a 25-acre historical site in the park that includes the lighthouse and a history center. In the center, the story of the lighthouse and its place in the history of the rugged shore of Lake Superior is told in a series of interesting displays.

Camping at Split Rock Lighthouse State Park is at dispersed campsites. There are two types of dispersed campsites. One type is at the cart-in campsite. In this style of camping, campers park their vehicles at the campground parking lot. They then pick up a lightweight cart, the use of which is included in the campsite fee. The cart is then loaded with camping gear and pulled to a preselected campsite. At this state park, the campsites are spread out above the shoreline and inland from 350 to 1,950 feet from the parking lot. There are 20 cart-in campsites.

The other dispersed campsites here are four backpacker campsites. These are spread out along the lakefront trail beyond the cart-in campsites.

Trails

Split Rock Lighthouse State Park has about eight miles of foot trails, six of which are also cross-country ski trails. The trails run along and above the lakeshore and through the largely hardwood forest on both sides of the North Shore Highway.

The Superior Hiking Trail is accessible from the park.

For a map and further information contact:
Park Manager
Split Rock Lighthouse State Park
2010A Highway 61 East
Two Harbors, MN 55616
(218) 226-3065

For Historic Site information, or Group Tour reservations:
Minnesota Historical Society
2010 Highway 61 East
Two Harbors, MN 55616
(218) 226-4372

TEMPERANCE RIVER STATE PARK

Temperance River State Park is located 81 miles Northeast of Duluth; and 23 miles southwest of Grand Marais. The river was first named *Kawimbash* an Ojibway name meaning "Deep Hollow." The name was later changed to Temperance because the mouth of the river does not have a bar. The highway map grid is P-7. Temperance River State Park has two camping areas with 50 semi-modern sites.

In the 133-acre park are six miles of clearly marked trails. Some are quite steep and rocky, so wear your hiking boots. In addition to several waterfalls and rapids, there is a scenic gorge with large potholes. This is excellent family hiking. In addition, the new Superior Hiking Trail, which will follow the North Shore from Duluth to the Canadian border, is accessible from the park.

For a map or further information contact:
Park Manager
Temperance River State Park
Box 33
Schroeder, MN 55613
(218) 663-7386

TETTEGOUCHE STATE PARK

Tettegouche State Park is located in Lake County, 4.5 miles northeast of Silver Bay on Highway 61. The highway map grid is O-8.

This new 4,691-acre North Shore state park now incorporates the old Baptism River State Park, the site of the highest waterfalls in Minnesota. Tettegouche State Park offers a variety of experiences to the hiker, which range from trail along the shores of Lake Superior to ridge walking on the Saw Tooth Mountains. The park has a mile-long shoreline on Lake Superior, and four inland lakes.

The park headquarters and North Shore interpretive center are located on the east side of the North Shore Highway, next to the Baptism River Highway Rest Area. The park has a 14-site campground.

At one time the Tettegouche State Park area was the site of a major logging operation. A logging camp was set up in what is now the west side of the park. The lumberjacks from the Canadian province of New Brunswick named the four local lakes after Algonquin Indian names for New Brunswick landmarks.

After a while, the logging camp was purchased by a group of Duluth businessmen as a sportsmen's camp. A succession of owners preserved the area until it was incorporated with Baptism River State Park as Tettegouche State Park.

Trails

High Falls Trail is a mile-long trail, passing under the Baptism River bridge and heading uphill in a northern direction to the site of the High Falls.

Shovel Point Trail is a continuation of the lakeside path that leads northeast to circle around Shovel Point, an impressive promontory jutting out into Lake Superior.

The other trails in this park are interconnected loop trails located west of the trailhead parking lot and also accessible from the west side of the park, off the Lax Lake Road parking area. Visitors leave their vehicles on the Lax Lake Road and walk into the park on a service road that leads to the old Tettegouche Camp. On the way to the camp, trails lead off from both sides of the service road. There is a trail that crossroads in the area of the old camp. These paths make up a connecting system of loop trails that circle around 13-acre Nicado, 50-acre Nipisiquit, 121-acre Mic Mac and 68-acre

Tettegouche lakes. Along these loops there are side trails that lead to ridgetop scenic viewpoints. These new trails have already made Tettegouche a favored state park for hikers.

Trails in the park allow access to the Superior Hiking Trail.

For a map and further information contact:

Tettegouche State Park Manager
474 Hwy. 61E.
Silver Bay, MN 55614
(218) 296-6157

TOWER-SOUDAN STATE PARK

Tower-Soudan State Park is located one mile west of Soudan on Highway 169. On the state highway map its grid location is M-7. The main attraction of this 1,300-acre park is in the underground tours through the now inactive iron mine, 2,341 feet underground. The temperature down in the mine is always 50 degrees, so you may want to wear a sweater or light jacket. Because of the rough conditions of the mine, long pants and walking shoes are recommended. Hard hats are provided. In addition to the walking tour there is a three quarter mile ride on an electric train. These tours, guided by former miners, give the visitor a look at Minnesota's oldest and deepest underground iron mine.

In the year 1892, more than 1800 miners removed over 570,000 tons of high grade iron ore from this mine. The mine continued operating until 1963. In 1965 United States Steel donated the mine and 1,200 surrounding acres to the state of Minnesota as a state park.

Above ground, there are nine miles of foot trails which pass by the sites of the Lake Vermillion 1866 gold rush as well as the old efforts of open-pit mining. Some of the easy walking trails are on abandoned railroad grades or roads. Wear a good pair of walking or running shoes on these trails. Here you can see the natural beauty of the park.

The park does not have a campground. Those who wish to stay in the area overnight could camp out at nearby Bear Head Lake State Park or stay at one of the area's fine resorts.

For a map and further information Contact:

Tower-Soudan State Park
P.O. Box 335
Soudan, MN 55782
(218) 353-2245

State Corridor Trails

In the Minnesota Arrowhead Region, the state corridor trails are the Arrowhead Trail, the Willard Munger Trail, the North Shore Trail, and the Taconite Trail. These tails are designated by the Minnesota Department of Natural Resources as multiple-use trails in principle, to provide recreation for snowmobilers, skiers, hikers, and horseback riders. In practice, however, for most of their length the trails in the Arrowhead Region have been strictly designed, constructed, and maintained as snowmobile trails.

The fact that much of the Arrowhead corridor trail system runs along drainage routes or through wetlands, combined with the lack of brushing along the trails, greatly restricts their use to winter recreational travel. In plain English, for most of their length the multiple use corridor trails of the Arrowhead Region, when not frozen and covered with snow, are too wet and/or brushy to be hiked.

The Fire and Willard Munger trails are the exceptions. One can find 14 mile section from Duluth to Carlton, and the 40 mile section from Barnum to Hinckley that are bituminous paved railroad grades and can be an easy hike when the trail is ice and snow free.

These two sections are used by the public as bike trails, as easy walking paths, and for snowmobiling. This is a good use of these abandoned grades, as Minnesota does not have many miles of off-the-road bike paths, or long, easy walking hiking trails.

Fire Trail, Barnum to Moose Lake

This section of the Munger Trail has been named the Fire Trail. During the forest fire of 1894 the trains on the railroad line was the main escape route that saved many people from the Hickley Fire.

Now the trail provides an excellent way for bikers, hikers, walkers, and snowmobilers to travel through forests and farm lands.

Munger State Trail
Duluth to Carlton Section

This great 14 mile paved trail from Duluth to Carlton is built on the roadbed of a Northern Pacific Railroad shortline. Starting from Duluth, the trailhead is southeast of Grand Avenue, at 69th Avenue West, between the Wildard Motel and the Indian Point Campground. There is a parking lot across from 69th avenue west from the trailhead. After paralleling Duluth's Western Waterfront for several miles, the trail crosses Grand Avenue on an old railroad bridge starts uphill on a one percent grade.

Enroute to Carlton the path cuts through interesting rock structures and offers well as outstanding views of the surrounding forested hills. At about mid-point there is a connection with both the west and east sides of Duluth's Mission Creek Trail, which starts at Fond Du Lac, near Duluth's far west and makes a loop up one side of Mission Creek and down the other. This is not a paved trail. Further on at Buffalo Valley a paved spur trail leads to a private campground and a concession stand that offers food and drink.

Near its western end, the trail edges the northern border of beautiful Jay Cooke State Park, and for a while it runs along the north shore of Forbay Lake, which provides water power for Minnesota Power. This is a good place to look for wildlife.

At the west end of Forbay Lake a side trail connects to the Jay Cooke State Park's trail system, ending near the park campground. Then you will pass over an old railroad bridge that spans the Saint Louis River, then, it is a short distance to where the trail ends near the railroad yard in Carlton.

This section of the Willard Munger Trail is generally considered to be more of a biking trail than a hiking trail. However, hikers do use it, and can make a nice five mile loop walk with the Western Waterfront Trail.

This trail holds much potential for Volkswalks, Volksbikes, and Volksskiing. In the future, this paved railroad grade may become the site of the Arrowhead Region's first year-round Volkssport event.

For further information contact:
Minnesota Department of Natural Resources
Trails and Waterways Unit
Information Center
Box 40, 500 Lafayette Road
St. Paul, MN 55146
(612) 1-800-652-9747 or
(612) 296-6699

Duluth Trails

"Give me the clear blue sky over my head, and the green turf beneath my feet, a winding road before me and a three hours' march to dinner-and then to thinking."

Willian Hazlitt, "On Going a Journey"

Duluth is a unique city. Not only is it surrounded on all sides by areas of natural beauty, but there are many outstanding scenic places within its boundaries. Many of these are in city parks that offer exceptional opportunities for the hiker to enjoy the varied facets of the northern forest.

These trails are for day use only. If you want to stay over night—for it will take several days to hike all of Duluth's trails—there are many good hotels and motels in the city. There should be no problem getting a room in the a weekdays. For a weekend stay, book your reservations about a month ahead of your trip.

For those who wish to stay at a campground, there is a campground at Indian Point and at Spirit Mountain.

Amity Creek Trails

To reach the Amity Creek Trail, take the road going north on the west side of the Lester River Bridge at Superior Street. This road follows the west branch of the Lester River, crossing the river at seven places-hence the name Seven Bridges Road. At the seventh bridge and the junction with the Sky Line Drive there is a parking lot.

From here a trail follows Amity Creek, a branch of the Lester River. This trail is the old Snively Boulevard, named after a mayor of Duluth. Because of washouts of roadways and bridges, the boulevard is now in the condition of a trail, and is used by hikers and cross-country skiers. A short distance after leaving the parking lot the trail crosses a ruined bridge. Here on the west side of the trail is a large plantation of red and scotch pine that was planted shortly after the disastrous forest fire of 1918 that wiped out Cloquet and came close to burning much of Duluth. This pine forest is called the Marshall Plantation, after a prominent Duluth family that once owned the land.

A short side trail goes through this pine stand, going back to the Skyline Drive and to connections with the Hawk Ridge trails. Walking this trail is an interesting experience. You should take note of the scarcity of plants under the pine canopy that makes it difficult for herbivorous animals and their predators to live there. Notice the alignment and spacing of the pines too. The picket fence effect is no longer favored for tree planting in recreation lands. Now trees are planted in a random pattern to give a more natural appearance.

Continuing on the Amity Creek Trail, you soon reach another washed out bridge, just below the confluence of the west and east branches of Amity Creek. Another trail branches off from here, going up the East Amity Creek, near the Jean Duluth Road. The main trail continues up the banks of the West Amity Creek, until it reaches an electrical power line. Recently the writer ran across a young bull moose on this part of the trail.

The trail then follows the power line back to the Skyline Drive,about a half-mile west of the starting place at the parking lot. This portion of the Amity Creek Trail is intersected at three points by loops of the Hawk Ridge trail system.

Bagley Nature Area, formerly Rock Hill Arboretum

This nature area is located on and below a rock ridge behind the University of Minnesota, Duluth Campus. This 32-acre tract of forested land contains a stream, a pond, and three miles of wood-chip-covered hiking trails. An interesting feature of the trail is in the use of old railroad ties in the construction of bridges and stairways. This is also the site of a former ski hill that was closed after the opening of Spirit Mountain.

The best way to walk these trails is to take Woodland Avenue, then turn left at St. Marie Street, then turn right onto Montrose Avenue. Take the first left turn that will take you into parking lot N. At the far end of the lot there is a seven-space public parking area. The rest of the lot is reserved for student parking for the nearby Oakland Apartments.

Under the direction of the University Life Sciences Department, the nature area is both an educational facility and an outdoor recreational resource. Although it is on campus and serves as a place of respite and inspiration for students, the nature area is open for all.

Chester Creek Nature Trail

This 2.2-mile-long trail starts at the Skyline Boulevard below the Chester Bowl Recreational Area. During the summer season, Chester Bowl offers picnicking and softball. In the winter, skiing is the main activity, with trails for Nordic skiing, and hills and jumps for Alpine skiing.

The Chester Creek Nature Trail is a rather rough hiking trail that runs along both sides of the Chester Creek ravine, from the recreation area to Fourth Street and 14th Avenue East.

Most of the trail is in the deep ravine of one of Duluth's 23 major streams that drain into Lake Superior. While in the ravine you are sheltered from the sights and sounds of the surrounding city and you may have the feeling of being in a remote, wild forest.

The trailhead is on the west side of the Chester Creek Bridge, and starts at a stairway down from the road to a wood-chipped trail beside Chester Creek. The trail begins in a grove of white pine. Standing among these noble trees, you are at the head of the Chester Creek ravine. This ravine becomes deeper and steeper farther downstream.

To prevent accidents it is wise to keep young children in hand while walking on the steeper sections of the trail, even though these have posts with safety cables.

As the trail follows Chester Creek downstream through a typical northern forest, it moves up and down the side of the ravine. At times the trail is at stream level and at other times it is high above Chester Creek.

City park crews have done a great deal of work to keep this and other park trails in good condition. Besides brushing vegetation and planking over wet areas and gullies, they have put in several new steel and concrete bridges over Chester Creek.

About halfway to Fourth Street the trail passes under the Eighth Street Bridge. From the west side of the bridge a stairway provides Eighth Street access to the trail.

Duluth's ravine parks provide important habitats for a wide range of wildlife species that include many birds, some of which nest in the parks, while others stop over as part of their migration. Small mammals also live in the ravines, and there are occasional sightings of larger animals such as deer, bear, and moose. It seems that the ravines are wildlife travel corridors.

Close to the Fourth Street Bridge there is a concrete stairway coming down to the trail from a steel and concrete scenic overlook.

Just upstream from the Fourth Street Bridge is one of two waterfalls that can be seen from along the trail.

The Fourth Street Bridge allows access to the trail on the east side of Chester Creek. Just above the bridge is the site of the homestead of Charles Chester, for whom the creek was named. Mr. Chester filed a claim on this property on May 31, 1856. There has not been much change in the ravine since then.

From the Chester homestead the trail returns to the Chester Bowl Recreational Area along the east side of the ravine.

Congdon Park Nature Trail

This beautiful little park is located at 31st Avenue East and Superior Street in the heart of the East Duluth residential district. The trail follows the Tischer Creek from Superior Street through a wild garden of trees, rocks, waterfalls, and pools, to Vermillion Road. Walking on this trail makes the visitor feel that he or she is in a forest instead of the center of a modern city.

Starting at the Superior Street Bridge, the main trail begins at the left side of the bridge and follows the creek upstream along the ridge to the Vermillion Road end of the trail. To see the canyons of Congdon Park, take the path going downhill that is just to the left of the west side of the bridge. This will take you down to the level of the creek. Going upstream, the creek is crossed by several steel and wood bridges that were put in place with the aid of a helicopter. This is the deepest section of the canyon. The red stone cliffs are very impressive. At the end of the canyon, the trail goes uphill to join the main trail.

The Duluth Junior League has set up station markers along the creek and printed a guidebook that has detailed information on each station. This guidebook is available at the Duluth Parks Department, ski shops, and some book stores.

Hartley Hill Trails

This 420-acre tract is located on the west side of Woodland Avenue, below Minneapolis Avenue. There is a gravel road into the area off Woodland Avenue. The road goes downhill and over a creek, to a parking place next to a small manmade pond. This pond is stocked with trout for children's fishing only.

Hartley Hill rises several hundred feet above the area, giving a view of forested hills and brushy lowlands. There are several miles of trails in Hartley Field that are used by hikers and cross-country skiers. At the present time these trails are not tied together, but future plans call for a three-mile-long trail system that will allow the walking visitor easy access to this interesting area.

Hawk Ridge Nature Reserve Trails

The Hawk Ridge Nature Reserve Trails are located one mile east of the junction of Glenwood Road and the Skyline Parkway. They were developed on city land by the Duluth Audubon Society. The society planned, constructed, and maintains these fine trails.

Hawk Ridge is one of the best locations in the United States to view the fall migration of hawks and eagles. It seems that the position of Lake Superior and other topographic and climatic factors tend to work together to make this area an aerial funnel in which these birds of prey ride air currents on their annual trip south. Mid-September to Mid-October is the best time to see the migrating birds.

Indian Point Campground

This convenient little campground is in Duluth's West End at 902 South 69th Avenue West, across the street from the Duluth Zoo. It is a 60-site, modern campground with electrical hookups for some sites.

The campground occupies a peninsula into the estuary of the Saint Louis River. This river was known to the Native Americans as *Kitchigumi-Zibi* or "Lake Superior River," the largest river that flows into Lake Superior. French explorers renamed the river Saint Louis after Louis XI, a famous French king who reigned during the Crusades.

Starting at Seven Beaver Lake, the river follows a crooked route for 160 miles before entering Lake Superior. This river drains a land area of 6,347 square miles. During the early years, the Saint Louis River was an important link in a water route from the Great Lakes to the Mississippi River valley.

Nothing is known of the early history of Indian Point Campground. It would seem that its location on a prominent peninsula on the Saint Louis River would have made it a good choice campsite for Native Americans, fur traders, and explorers who traveled the river by canoe.

Records show that between the years 1911 and 1916 the Duluth Park Department purchased 39.63 acres from several private landowners and the State of Minnesota for $27,166.

There must have been some recreational use of the point prior to the park deparment's purchase, for when the campground was being prepared for the first public use in the spring of 1926, records show an office building, a pavilion, a caretaker's house, and restrooms to be already on the site.

In 1926 the Duluth Parks Department had two campgrounds. Besides the one at Indian Point, there was also the Brighton Beach Campground, located in eastern Duluth near the mouth of the Lester River. The EPA National Water Laboratory is now located there.

In addition, the city operated a campground in the bowl area of Chester Park for a time. The Duluth Curling Club building also saw service as an indoor campground.

In the fall of 1926, the Duluth newspaper reported that 20,000 people in 5,000 automobiles had camped at Indian Point Campground. By 1930 the campground was showing a profit. In the same year, a comfort station, showers, and laundry facilities were built at a cost of $6,000. In addition, two cabins were constructed by the Woodruff Lumber Company, paid for out of campground receipts.

In 1931 a park department report suggested that the drop in the numbers of visitors to Indian Point Campground that year was due to a shortage of cabin space. The report stated that people wanted to stay in cabins and were no longer content to haul tents and cots to the campground. The suggestion was followed that year with the construction of three more cabins.

In 1933, due to a lack of funds, the Duluth City Council voted to close Indian Point Campground and move its cabins to the Brighton Beach Campground. This move appears to have been reversed before it was implemented, for in that year a Mr. J. Brown leased the campground for 10 percent of the gross. This arrangement was used for two decades.

In 1934 three more cabins were constructed at Indian Point.

In 1942, after the entrance of the United States into World War II, there was a slight drop in campground revenue. However, business soon picked up as the public began to save gasoline ration stamps in order to travel to Duluth and the North Shore.

Indian Point Campground also became a place to live for many war workers who were employed at local shipyards and in other war related industries. According to Duluth Park Department records, seven buildings were erected at Indian Point in 1943 for use by the Minnesota State Guard, who protected shipyards and other vital areas. Following the end of the war, however, very little was done to maintain or improve the campground.

146

In December of 1963, Duluth Mayor George D. Johnson urged the reactivation of Indian Point Campground. This was due in part to the closing of the campground at Brighton Beach to make way for the new federal water laboratory.

Shortly afterwards, Mr. Ray E. Hammer, Field Director of the National Campers and Hikers of America, recommended changes for Indian Point Campground. Among the changes were that the old cabins be removed, that a fulltime attendant be employed, a camp information board be erected, that each campsite have a parking space, and that the name of the campground be changed to Spirit Campground, after the nearby lake in the Saint Louis River.

In 1964 the old cabins were removed along with dead trees, and the grounds were cleared of brush.

In 1965 Indian Point Campground was reactivated. Within three years it was recognized as a major Duluth visitor attraction.

In 1970, money from the U.S. Bureau of Outdoor Recreation, plus matching funds from the Minnesota Department of Natural Resources and the City of Duluth resulted in the construction of a new building to house sanitary facilities and the campground office. The old caretaker's house was removed and the former sanitation building was cleared out for use as storage space.

In 1980, the Lake Superior Basin Studies Center of the University of Minnesota, Duluth, leased the management of Indian Point Campground for the purpose of research and student training. This arrangement lasted for several years. At the present time the campground is operated under a lease arrangement similar to those of the past and is very successful in providing for the needs of the camping public.

It is a good place for bicyclists, runners, and walkers to camp here, because the campground is very near both the Western Waterfront Trail and the Munger State Trail. The Western Waterfront Trail goes around the perimeter of the campground. The campground is on one side of the trail and the Saint Louis River is on the other side. The tree shaded trail around Indian Point Campground passes by several wildlife habitats and makes a great path for a nature hike. It is very popular with campers as well as area residents.

Kingsbury Creek Nature Trail

The creek is named after William Wallace Kingsbury, a prominent Duluthian who was a Minnesota territorial representative in the U.S. Congress from 1857 to 1858. He held land in the area and built a cabin along the creek.

The starting point for the 1.3-mile trail is at the northeast corner of the Duluth Zoo, just above the picnic area at the place where the Old Thompson Hill Road passes under a railroad bridge.

On the other side of the bridge there is a Y in the road. The left branch follows the creek upstream. The most noticeable tree here is the noble eastern white pine. The dark bark, long cones, and its five-to-a-bundle needles make the tree easy to spot. Notice that as the white pine becomes older its bark changes from smooth to furrowed.

Further uphill there is a crossroad. The road to the left goes over Kingsbury Creek Bridge and becomes a trail. The road to the right is the Old Thompson Hill Road, which in the past provided the people of Proctor with direct access to the Duluth Zoo area.

The Kingsbury Creek Trail lies straight ahead along the creek's flood plain. Plants that grow on these flood plains are often of great value to wildlife as food. This is demonstrated by the numerous signs of wildlife that can be seen on the soft soils of the flood plains compared to nearby areas.

Coming up out of the creek bottom, the trail goes uphill and onto the road, then takes a left turn and crosses a bridge over Kingsbury Creek. After crossing the bridge the trail turns uphill into a loop. Take the left side of the loop. The forest here is mainly paper birch, or as it is sometimes called, canoe birch, and aspen. The bark of the aspen, in contrast to the white birch, is off-white to greenish in color.

The Native Americans used birch bark for covering canoes and shelters and making various types of containers. Aspen was often used for its medicinal properties.

Birch and aspen are called pioneer species because they colonize a site after fire or logging. Then, through the process of plant succession, the short-lived birch and aspen are replaced by other trees such as fir, spruce, and pine.

Further along, where the trail turns to follow the creek back downstream, there are a number of northern white cedar trees. These are small shaggy, bark tree that has small, flat needles. The French-Canadian voyageurs called this tree *Arborvitae*, or "tree of life," because tea made from it acted to prevent scurvy. The needles and twigs of the white cedar are one of the most favored winter foods of the white-tailed deer. The trees are often browsed as high as the deer can reach.

There are some very scenic overlooks of the surrounding countryside from the high points of the trail. In following Kingsbury Creek downstream, the trail allows the hiker to see the many different plants that grow along the creek bed as well as the many species of birds that can be found on this stretch of the trail.

Back at the bridge, the trail is now on the Old Thompson Hill Road heading back to the starting point. This area is evidently good white-tailed deer habitat, as there are many tracks on the soft surface of the road. What seems to be part of the attraction is the abundance of plants such as sumac and alder that provide the deer with excellent browse.

The Kingsbury Creek Nature Trail has so many interesting sights that walkers should be sure to allow enough time to experience all that it offers.

For Futher information contact
Duluth Department of Parks and Recreation
308 City Hall
Duluth,MN
(218) 723-3337

Lester Park Trails

Lester Park is located at 61st Avenue East and Superior Street, where the two branches of the Lester River come together. The East and West Lester Rivers form the east and west boundaries of the park.

The Lester River was named after the original homesteder. The Indian name for the river was *Bus-Ka-Bika-zibi* which means "River where the water flows through a worn place in the rocks."

The mouth of the Lester River is a favored place to net smelt. Every spring, between the middle of April and the first of May, smelt move up the North Shore streams to spawn. Smelt are small, silvery saltwater fish that were planted in the Great Lakes by the Michigan Conservation Department in the early part of this century. The effects of this exotic species on the native fish stocks is, to this day a subject of controversy.

Smelt first attracted the attention of fishermen here in the late 1940's. For the last 40 years people from all over the upper midwest have been making springtime pilgrimages to Duluth and the North Shore during the smelt run.

The Lester River mouth is also a fovored place for anglers to try for native trout as well as Atlantic and Pacific Ocean salmon.

Lester Park's main entrance is on the east side of the Lester River Bridge, off of the Lester River Road. Next to the parking lot there is a foot bridge that leads to the picnic grounds.

The river valley trails that line both branches of the Lester River are connected by cross country trails, making an interesting network.

Lincoln Park Nature Trail

Lincoln Park is in West Duluth between 25th Avenue West and 26th Avenue West. Its south border is 3rd Street and the north border is the Skyline Boulevard.

This 37.4-acre park is one of Duluth's oldest. First construction was started in 1890.

Each Duluth park trail has a distinctive loop. The one-and-a-half-mile loop trail in Lincoln Park goes up the east side of Miller Creek and comes down the west side. Even though the trail is quite short and in the middle of a residential area, the park is quite scenic and in many places it has the appearance of a wild mountain trail.

The trail starts near the Third Street entrance at the park pavilion by the picnic area. An unusual feature is a large glacier formed rock outcropping painted to look like an elephant. The trail crosses Miller Creek on a stone bridge. It then crosses the parkway and heads up the east side of the stream. The trail has an average grade of about 8 percent; some sections have stairways.

At places, the creek valley becomes a deep and scenic gorge with overlooks and picnic facilities nearby. Near a bridge a dangerous area of falls is protected by a cyclone fence.

After passing under the 10th Street Bridge by a series of waterfalls, the trail traverses a rocky section, then ascends a stone staircase and runs up into the woods. A short distance further on, the trail crosses the Miller Creek on a park bridge and returns to the starting point along the west side of the creek.

Mission Creek Nature Trail

The Mission Creek Trail is located in the community of Fond du Lac at the western edge of Duluth. Fond du Lac are French words that in English mean Head of the Lake. This denotes its location at the extreme western end of Lake Superior

In 1680's the French explorer, Daniel Greysolon du Lhut, the namesake of the city of Duluth met with native leaders here in an effort to bring peace to the region. Warfare between the Native American tribes was very harmful to the French fur trade.

In the 1800's, because of its location on the Saint Louis River that was a water route connection between the Great Lakes and Mississippi River, Fond du Lac became the site of several important fur trading posts.

Mission Creek Trail is named after a Fond du Lac Ojibway mission and school directed by the Reverend Edmund F. Ely. It was in operation from 1834 to 1839.

The trail is a 4.25 miles long loop and is generally in good to fair hiking condition. However, it is rough trail and hiking boots are needed for this trail. A full canteen and a hikers lunch will help make the hike more enjoyable.

In order to have enough time to experience all that Mission Creek has to offer allow yourself the better part of a day to hike this trail.

The Trail

The west side of Mission Creek Nature Trail was first constructed as a auto parkway complete with a number of stone and concrete bridges over the numerous crossing of Mission Creek. But the expense of maintenance of this stream side road proved to be too costly and after a series of cloudbursts washed out large sections of road the parkway as abandoned.

The east side of the trail was probably used by Native Americans as a trail to their maple sugar camps and later as a road used by the early settlers.

To reach the Mission Creek Trail follow Highway 23 west to the community of Fond du Lac. The trail starts in a open field at the end of 131st Avenue West, where there is ample parking space. Downstream from a catch dam on Mission Creek is a trail sign pointing towards where the Mission Creek Trail crosses the creek. After crossing the creek the trail swings west to parallel Highway 210 before turning north along Mission Creek.

The lowland forest here is made up of moisture tolerant trees such as willow, elm, ash, and aspen with an understory of spruce. In time the hardwood species will give way to the spruce. As the trail moves up to higher, drier soils the forest is made up of mainly birch and aspen.

Along the trail there are exposures of the two billion year old Fond du Lac sandstone. This brown sandstone was quarried from several sites in this part of Duluth. It was used extensively for local construction in the 1880's.

After crossing over the last of the old parkway bridges the trail climbs up the side of the creek valley past a stand of white pine and white spruce. After the trail levels off you reach a concrete bridge that crosses over the paved Willard Munger State Corridor Trail. From this place on the trail, there is an excellent view of Duluth's rocky ridgeline.

Two prominent crags stand out above the ridge. The one on the left is Ely Peak; the other is Bardon's Peak

Ely Peak was named after the Reverend Edmund F. Ely, the missionary at Fond du Lac.

For many years Ely Peak was the site of Ojibway Comming-of-Age Ceremonies for the boys entering manhood. A candidate would climb to the summit where he would lie on a large flat rock for five days without food or water. At the end of this time his parents would take him water. If he could last another five days, he had passed the test and was considered a warrior. During his ten day fast he would expect to receive visions of his future life.

According to another Indian legend there was a wild man who lived on this peak. He could be seen roaming about dressed in a blue cap and red leggings and carrying a new gun. Watch for him!

Bardon's Peak is named after a Kentuckian who once owned the land. The Indians called it Manitoushgebik meaning "Spirit Mountain." The Spirit Mountain recreational complex located just east of here takes its name from the peak.

Part of the legend of this place was that it was the camping place of Naniboujou, an Native American demigod who, among his many feats, created the Apostle Islands in Wisconsin by throwing a handful of earth at his rival Ah-Mik, the beaver spirit who dominated Kitchi-Gami. (Lake Superior)

From the level of the deck of the bridge the Mission Creek Trail moves down to the Munger Trail and turns to right (east) in the direction of Duluth. After traveling a short distance on the Munger Trail there is a trail sign pointing the way back to the Mission Creek Trail along the east side of the Mission Creek.

This part of the trail can be very wet after a rain. The forest of this part of the trail is made up of highland hardwood trees such as basswood, oak and maple. There are areas of sugar maple, the sap of which is used to make maple sugar, in the past an important food staple of the Native American diet. The Ojibway people had a number of sugar camps here.

During the late 1860's a mail carrier from Duluth with a packsack of mail bound for the community of Fond du Lac was lost for twelve hours in a maze of trails around the sugar camp area. He finally found his way out of the woods by climbing a tree to get his bearings.

About half way down this side of the trail there is the trace of a road going to the left (east). This is known by some of the local residents as the Ghost Town Road. So far this writer has been unable to uncover the meaning of this name.

As the Mission Creek Trail returns to its starting point it passes through stands of spruce and fir trees. This is a wet area of deep gullies that are crossed by bridges and planking.

The Mission Creek Trail is the most primitive trail in the Duluth parks trail system. Its route passes through a wild forest that is home for deer, moose, bear, and other wildlife including many species of birds.

Park Point Trail

Park Point or Minnesota Point the long sand spit that separates the Duluth-Superior harbor from the open waters of Lake Superior was called *Shaga-wa-mik* by the Chippewa Indians which meant "long narrow point of land." It is one of the most unique places in Minnesota. It is also the longest fresh water sand bar in the world.

According to indian legend, Park Point was created by the Great Spirit. It happened when a young Chippewa brave was trapped on what is now the Wisconsin side of the bay by a Sioux hunting party. The young brave faced certain death from either the Sioux or the icy waters of Kitchi-Gami. At this point the Great Spirit took pity on his plight and urged him into the frigid waters. As the pursued brave dashed into the bay, land formed under his racing feet to create a long sandy point. The Sioux who followed close were close behind when the Great Spirit caused part of the newly formed land to be swept into the lake, thus cutting off the chase. The gap is now known as the Superior entry. The Chippewa youth continued his way to the area now known as Duluth without getting his feet wet.

The geologist's version is that Minnesota Point is largely a deposit of sand created by the prevailing northwest winds.

The Trail

The Park point Trail starts at the Sky Harbor Airport at the end of Minnesota Avenue. After passing through a pedestrian gap in a fence, the trail is on a road along side of the airport runway. After a short distance a trail leads off to the left and enters a wooded area where there is the forested trail to the Superior entry end of Park Point.

The point is a bird sanctuary. Because its location on Lake Superior and its vegetative cover Park Point attracts many species of birds. It is nationally known as a place to look at birds.

Among the large red and white pine are patches of strawberries, raspberries and blueberries. But some are well guarded by large areas of poison ivy, so beware.

About half way down Park Point the trail crosses the pumping station of the Lake Superior-Cloquet water line. Beyond this point the trail continues theough the forest. This part of the point was once the location of many summer homes and several private clubs. These were abandoned after the second World War.

At the end of the deep woods there is a steel tower that is used as a triangulation station used for Lake Superior survey work. From here on the trail is more open and sandy, making walking more strenuous. A short distance further on is the ruins of the old Park Point Lighthouse. It was built in 1858 at a cost of $15,000. It is now only two-thirds of its orginal height. It was constructed of brick manufactured in Cleveland, Ohio. It lens came from the Bardon Company of Paris, France. In 1878 the lens was removed and palced in the lighthouse at the west side of the Lake Superior side of the Superior entry where it remains today.

The home of Duluths first permanent resident, George Stuntz was located near the site of the lighthouse in 1855. Stuntz was a famous pioneer surveyor who left his mark on many places in the Arrowhead Country. Past the old lighthouse is a very large concrete building on the harbor side of the point that was used for small craft construction and by the Corps of Enginners for buoy storage.

From this point it is a short walk to the Superior entry where all manner of vessels pass from the wide open lake to the sand bar protected Duluth Superior harbor.

From the hiker can either return by way of the trail or by way of the lake side sandy beach where you have a magnificent view of Lake Superior and the spectaclar east Duluth skyline.

Western Waterfront Trail

This popular trail starts at a signed parking lot across Grand Avenue from the Duluth Zoo, next to the Tappa Keg Inn. The trail now ends at the community of Riverside, two and a half miles away.

Although Duluth is well known as a Lake Superior city, it is also a Saint Louis River city. The fact is that more of Duluth is along the riverfront than along the lakeshore.

The Saint Louis River is the largest Minnesota river that drains into Lake Superior.

Not much is known about the early history of the lower Saint Louis River. It can be assumed that through the years a number of Native American tribes passed through the estuary area, stopping for a while because of the abundant natural resources.

The first white man on record to have visited the Saint Louis River, in the year 1679, was Daniel de Greysolon, Sieur Duluth, the person for whom the city of Duluth was named. The purpose of his journey is said to have been to improve conditions for French fur traders by trying to end Native American tribal warfare that was very damaging to the fur trade.

The lower Saint Louis River was part of the transportation route of the fur trade. It was an entrepot for the movement of trade goods and furs between the Great Lakes and the Mississippi River Valley.

Over a period of time, a number of fur trading posts were established by French, British, and American fur companies along the lower Saint Louis River to take advantage of its location.

Because most travel was by watercraft, trails were not developed along the lower Saint Louis River. The first important land transportation route along this section of the river was the Lake Superior and Mississippi Railroad connecting St. Paul to Duluth. It was completed in 1870. Later the track was acquired by the Burlington Northern Railroad, then in 1977 the railroad gave the right of way to the city of Duluth. Now, part of it the right of way has been developed as the Western Waterfront Trail.

The track is now being used by the nonprofit Lake Superior and Mississippi Railroad for a 12 mile tourist railroad. Regular departures start from a parking lot next to the Western Waterfront Trail parking lot. The train runs every Saturday and Sunday at 11:00 am, 1:30 pm, and 4:00 pm, from July to September. For more information call (218) 727-8025.

The Trail

The Western Waterfront Trail came into being to allow public access to an outstanding outdoor recreational area while preserving its natural values.

The trail is 8 feet wide and covered with crushed limestone, suitable for walking or biking. Motorized travel is not permitted.

The trail crosses creeks, goes around Indian Point Campground, passes by several types of wildlife habitats, and ends near a shipyard site that built ships in both World Wars in the community of Riverside. At Riverside the hiker can retrace his steps or turn right on Spring Street and walk to the paved Munger State Trail, then, turn right (east) to return to a couple of blocks west of the Western Waterfront parking lot. Turning left (west) on the Munger State Trail will point you toward the city of Carlton, which is about 10 miles away.

Future plans call for the Western Waterfront Trail to be extended west past its present terminus of Riverside to the community of Fond Du Lac. Another leg of the trail is now being extented east to 63rd avenue west, or more. This would increase the length of the trail to 10 miles.

But, for the time being, there are plenty of things to see from the existing trail. Three hundred species of birds have been identified in the area. Fourteen species of mammals live in several habitats ranging from marshlands to dry hills. To see the wildlife, walk slowly and stop often. Remaining still for a while will greatly increase your chances.

For brochures and other information on Duluth park trails contact:

Duluth Parks and Recreation
308 City Hall
Duluth, MN 55802
(218) 723-3337

Volkssports

Volkssports, or Peoples' Sports, are noncompetitive sports activities featuring the vigorous exercises of walking, biking, cross-country skiing, and swimming. Many families take part in Volkssports events because these are activities in which people of all ages can participate.

One of the Volkssports is Volksmarching, Which translated into English means "Peoples' Walk." It was imported to the United States from West Germany by returning United States military and civilian personnel who wanted to continue the Volkssports program in the United States.

Today, the American Volkssports Association or (AVA) has many local clubs. These clubs are part of state associations that serve to coordinate local club events to prevent scheduling conflicts.

You are not required to become a club member, or pay any fee to participate in any event. To take part in a Volksmarch all you have to do is to show up on time at the event starting point. You then pick up a free start card and start walking along a signed route. Your start card is marked at checkpoints along the route. Walkers are provided with a free drink at the checkpoints.

While most Volksmarchers walk at their own pace, others would rather run than walk. In some areas where there are several local clubs it is possible to take part in two or three events in a weekend.

Walking or hiking Volksmarches are held along scenic loop trails so that walkers finish at the place where they started. These foot events are usually on routes of 10 and 20 kilometers (6 and 12 miles). Cross-country ski and biking events are also held along scenic loop routes. But these may vary in distance. Swimming events are held in pools and are measured in pool laps. All events are free.

People who complete Volkssports events may elect to purchase medallions and other memorabilia. Some longtime Volksmarchers have huge collections of medals, plates, mugs, and other awards to show for their efforts.

A walker can also earn AVA milestone awards for distance walked or number of events. A milestone award is a pin, patch, and certificate in recognition of achievement. These awards are also optional.

As of January 1989, there are no year-round AVA events in the Arrowhead region.

For further information contact:
THE AMERICAN WANDERER
Suite 203, Phoenix Square
1001 Pat Booker Road
Universal City, Texas 78148
(512) 659-2112

Minnesota State Volkssport Association
Sharon Peterson
5131 University Ave N.E. #101
Columbia Height, MN 55421
(612) 572-9365

For More Information—

For Superior National Forest
Forest Supervisor
U.S. Forest Service
Box 338
Duluth, MN 55801
218-727-6692

Minnesota Department of Natural
    Resources
Box 44- Centennial Building
Saint Paul, MN 55155
612-296-4491
800-652-9747

Isle Royale National Park
Superintendent
Isle Royal National Park
87 N. Ripley St.
Houghton, MI 49931
906-482-3310

Voyageurs National Park
Superintendent
Voyageurs National Park
P.O. Box 50-A,
International Falls, MN 56649
218-283-9821

Minnesota Arrowhead
320 West 2nd Street #707
Duluth, MN 55802
218-723-4692

Index